T0090669

Praise for *Meditations on Living, Dying, and Loss*

"The translation is beautifully clear. This glimpse into the extraordinary intricacy of Buddhism shows how a major Tibetan text addressed the needs of both the living and the dead."

—*Publishers Weekly*

Praise for *The Tibetan Book of the Dead*

"Carrying out the first complete translation of this cycle of teachings has been an extraordinary accomplishment. I hope that the profound insights contained in this work will be a source of inspiration and support to many interested people around the world, as they have been in my own culture."

—His Holiness the Dalai Lama

"This is an event. A new and comprehensive translation of one of the seminal works of Tibetan Buddhism. His Holiness the Dalai Lama's substantive introduction provides a solid framework for understanding the nature of consciousness and personal identity."

—Richard Gere

"Magnificent . . . beautiful verse meditations."

—*The Guardian* (London)

"This famous cycle of sacred instructions and practices from the heart of the ancient Buddhist tradition of Tibet throws light on the innermost nature of the mind and forms an extraordinary guide to the experiences of life, dying, death, and rebirth. Profound and unique, it is one of the great treasures of wisdom in the spiritual heritage of humanity." —Sogyal Rinpoche, author of *The Tibetan Book of Living and Dying*

"This new translation of *The Tibetan Book of the Dead* is a tremendous accomplishment. The whole text is a vast source of inspiration."

—Francesca Fremantle, *Buddhadharma* magazine

PENGUIN BOOKS

MEDITATIONS ON LIVING, DYING, AND LOSS

GRAHAM COLEMAN is the president of the Orient Foundation (UK), a major Tibetan cultural conservancy organization. Writer/director of the acclaimed feature documentary *Tibet: A Buddhist Trilogy* and editor of the *Handbook of Tibetan Culture*, he has been editing Tibetan Buddhist poetry and prose texts in cooperation with various distinguished Tibetan masters and translators since the mid-1970s.

THUPTEN JINPA, PH.D., is the senior translator to His Holiness the Dalai Lama and president of the Institute of Tibetan Classics. His works include the translation of twelve books by the Dalai Lama, including the *New York Times* bestseller *Ethics for the New Millennium* and *The Universe in a Single Atom*, the Dalai Lama's perspective on the meeting of Buddhism and modern science.

GYURME DORJE, PH.D., is a leading scholar of the Nyingma tradition of Tibetan Buddhism. His seven major publications include works on Tibetan lexicology, medicine, divination, and pilgrimage guides to Tibet and Bhutan as well as the translations of HH Dudjom Rinpoche's *The Nyingma School of Tibetan Buddhism*.

MEDITATIONS ON LIVING, DYING, AND LOSS

The Essential Tibetan Book of the Dead

From the first complete translation of
The Tibetan Book of the Dead
Introductory Commentary by His Holiness the Dalai Lama

Selected and Introduced by GRAHAM COLEMAN
Translated by GYURME DORJE
Edited by GRAHAM COLEMAN *with* THUPTEN JINPA

PENGUIN BOOKS

PENGUIN BOOKS

Published by the Penguin Group
Penguin Group (USA) Inc., 375 Hudson Street, New York, New York 10014, U.S.A.
Penguin Group (Canada), 90 Eglinton Avenue East, Suite 700, Toronto,
Ontario, Canada M4P 2Y3 (a division of Pearson Penguin Canada Inc.)
Penguin Books Ltd, 80 Strand, London WC2R 0RL, England
Penguin Ireland, 25 St Stephen's Green, Dublin 2, Ireland (a division of Penguin Books Ltd)
Penguin Group (Australia), 250 Camberwell Road, Camberwell,
Victoria 3124, Australia (a division of Pearson Australia Group Pty Ltd)
Penguin Books India Pvt Ltd, 11 Community Centre, Panchsheel Park, New Delhi – 110 017, India
Penguin Group (NZ), 67 Apollo Drive, Rosedale, North Shore 0632,
New Zealand (a division of Pearson New Zealand Ltd)
Penguin Books (South Africa) (Pty) Ltd, 24 Sturdee Avenue, Rosebank, Johannesburg 2196, South Africa

Penguin Books Ltd, Registered Offices: 80 Strand, London WC2R 0RL, England

First published in the United States of America by Viking Penguin,
a member of Penguin Group (USA) Inc. 2009
Published in Penguin Books 2010

Translation copyright © The Orient Foundation (UK) and Gyurme Dorje, 2005
Editorial apparatus copyright © The Orient Foundation (UK), Graham Coleman, and Thupten Jinpa, 2005
Introductory commentary copyright © His Holiness The Dalai Lama, 2005
Introduction and essays copyright © Graham Coleman, 2008
All rights reserved

Text selected from *The Tibetan Book of the Dead*, translated by Gyurme Dorje and
edited by Graham Coleman with Thupten Jinpa (Viking Penguin, 2006).

Illustrations by Robert Beer. Copyright © Robert Beer, 1999, 2008.

THE LIBRARY OF CONGRESS HAS CATALOGED THE HARDCOVER EDITION AS FOLLOWS:
Karma-glin-pa, 14th cent.
[Bar do thos grol. English. Selections]
Meditations on living, dying, and loss : the essential Tibetan book of the dead / introductory
commentary by His Holiness the Dalai Lama; selected and introduced by Graham Coleman;
translated by Gyurme Dorje; edited by Graham Coleman with Thupten Jinpa.
p.   cm.
Translated from the Tibetan.
Includes bibliographical references.
ISBN 978-0-670-02128-4 (hc.)
ISBN 978-0-14-311813-8 (pbk.)
1. Intermediate state—Buddhism—Early works to 1800.   2. Death—Religious aspects—Buddhism—Early
works to 1800.   3. Spiritual life—Buddhism—Early works to 1800.   I. Padma Sambhava, ca. 717–ca. 762.
II. Coleman, Graham.   III. Gyurme Dorje.   IV. Thupten Jinpa.   V. Title.
BQ4490.K37213 2009
294.3'423—dc22   2009028764

Set in Adobe Caslon • *Designed by Alissa Amell*

146122990

Contents

Acknowledgments

From the moment in 1988, when I first tentatively suggested to HH the Dalai Lama the idea of preparing a first complete translation of *The Tibetan Book of the Dead*, the Dalai Lama kindly gave his continuous support to our project throughout our fifteen years of work. At the very beginning, he made a request to HH Dilgo Khyentse Rinpoche, one of the most revered twentieth-century masters of Tibetan Buddhism, to give an oral commentary to me on key sections of *The Tibetan Book of the Dead*. The Dalai Lama knew that three of the twelve chapters of this compendium of texts had been translated by Lama Kazi Dawa Samdup and W. Y. Evans-Wentz in 1927, but that no one had translated the entire volume. Dilgo Khyentse Rinpoche graciously agreed to the Dalai Lama's request, and over a period of four weeks Khyentse Rinpoche gave an incisive and illuminating oral commentary on core elements of this cycle of teachings. Each day these commentaries were eloquently translated by Sogyal Rinpoche.

While in Kathmandu receiving the oral commentary from Khyentse Rinpoche, I was fortunate to meet Dr. Gyurme Dorje, who had previously translated Longchen Rabjampa's commentary on the *Guhya-garbha Tantra*, the root text on which *The Tibetan Book of the Dead* is based. During our first meeting, Gyurme agreed to make a new annotated translation of the entire *Tibetan Book of the Dead*, a task he has undertaken with exceptional care and dedication. While Gyurme was working on the translation he was also employed at the School of Oriental and African Studies in London as a research fellow, translating into English *An Encyclopedic Tibetan–Chinese Dictionary.*

During this time, Gyurme worked closely with the highly regarded scholar Zenkar Rinpoche, who is one of the foremost contemporary lineage holders of *The Tibetan Book of the Dead*. Zenkar Rinpoche kindly advised Gyurme throughout the translation of our text and also gave an extensive oral commentary to us on the extract included here under the title "Uncovering the Nature of Mind."

At various stages of the project, the Dalai Lama answered my questions about difficult points and also dictated to me the lucid and succinct introductory commentary on the complete translation, an extract from which is included here under the title "Exploring the Notion of Continuity of Consciousness." At the Dalai Lama's request, Khamtrul Rinpoche, also a lineage holder of the *Tibetan Book of the Dead* cycle of teachings, gave a beautiful oral commentary on the extract titled here "Body and Mind Dissolving."

Throughout the process of editing the complete translation, I had the good fortune of working with Geshe Thupten Jinpa, senior translator to the Dalai Lama, whom I had first met in 1977 and who has been a close friend since 1989 when he came to England to study philosophy at Cambridge. Jinpa translated the Dalai Lama's introduction and reviewed every line and word of my draft edited translation with me twice, in the course of which he made countless important and inspiring suggestions. Everyone who knows Jinpa's work is aware of his special talent both as a translator and writer, and these have played an invaluable role in this project.

The selections included in this volume all come from our first complete translation of *The Tibetan Book of the Dead*. I feel deeply privileged to have been able to craft this new translation, founded on the kindness, patience, wisdom, and skill of HH the Dalai Lama, HH Dilgo Khyentse Rinpoche, Zenkar Rinpoche, and Khamtrul Rinpoche, together with my colleagues Gyurme Dorje and Thupten Jinpa.

Much of my work over the last thirty years would not have been possible without the lifelong friendship of the Orient Foundation's chairman, David Lascelles. It is difficult to thank him enough for all that he has made possible, beginning with our work together on the making of our film *Tibet: A Buddhist Trilogy*, in the 1970s, and ever since. Two other special friends, Elinore Detiger and Elsie Walker, made it possible for the translation of the complete *Tibetan Book of the Dead* to be initiated, and their kindness and confidence, together with that of Michael Baldwin, will not be forgotten. My sincere appreciation goes also to Johnnie and Buff Chace, Lucinda Ziesing, Faith Bieler, Lavinia Currier, Cynthia Jurs, Catherine Cochran, Margot Wilkie, Basil Panzer, Bokara Patterson, and Lindsay Masters for their important contributions to the early stages of this work.

My heartfelt thanks goes out also to the artist Robert Beer for his exquisite line drawings which illustrate the text, to Pip Heywood and Peter Le Blond for their kindness in critically reviewing my introductions to each chapter, and to Andrew Bell for his careful and generous editing and proofreading of the manuscript.

GRAHAM COLEMAN
2008, Bath, England

Padmasambhava (Guru Rinpoche)

Editor's Introduction

It is of course ironic, after only recently finishing fifteen years of work editing the first complete translation of *The Tibetan Book of the Dead*, that I am now writing the introduction to extracts from the complete text.

Needless to say, I dearly hope that our complete translation will always be the edition which will be referred to by those wishing to study this masterful text in its entirety, but when our editor at Penguin Books suggested that we consider creating this shorter, specifically focused volume, I was happy to do so.

The complete translation is a detailed and comprehensive compendium of texts, often composed in verse, which includes an array of practices for cultivating a deeper understanding of our own nature and psychological experience. It also presents one of the most compelling visions of the after-death state in world literature, a penetrating insight into the process of dying, and a transforming perspective on bereavement. Although few works on these subjects have the poetic elegance and inspirational potency of *The Tibetan Book of the Dead*, the complete work does contain material specific to practitioners of this cycle of teachings, while other sections are interlaced with the folklore of ancient Tibet and are not directly relevant to our lives today.

In this volume, therefore, my aim is to present many of the most beautifully written passages of the complete translation and to draw out those of its central perspectives and insights that are the most relevant to our modern experience.

In creating our first complete translation, our intention was to present the entire work in a way that, as honestly as we could, reflected the insights and intentions of the Tibetan masters of this cycle of teachings, and also to maintain the moving, poetic beauty of the original work. In order to do this, as is described in the acknowledgments, the complete translation was based on the oral commentarial explanation of contemporary lineage holders and was carried out with the continual advice of contemporary masters. I have therefore not changed the line-by-line translation of the extracts included in this volume, although I have removed the annotations that accompany the complete translation so as to enhance the directness and readability of the extracts selected. In consultation with Thupten Jinpa, I have also extracted the early sections of the Dalai Lama's introductory commentary on the first complete translation so that this now focuses on exploring the notion of continuity of consciousness, and in the chapter titled "Wisdoms, Elements, and Subtle Energies" I have blended together two practices in order to succinctly reveal the meaning of the complex symbolism related to our mental and sensory processes.

Since the first publication of extracts from *The Tibetan Book of the Dead* in 1927, our understanding of the philosophy and practices relating to this magnificent cycle of teachings has deepened profoundly and brought the contemporary relevance of its insights into ever sharper focus. We now have a much expanded knowledge of the symbolism through which the understandings related to the nature of consciousness and human experience are presented, we now understand the subtle meditative techniques used as the vehicle for exploring the nature of our mental and sensory processes, and we have a deeper knowledge of the origins of the text. In selecting the extracts for this volume, I have tried to present those sections of the complete translation that most directly address the deepening of our insight into our own psychological habits and perspectives, our understanding of the process of dying and the nature of the after-death state, and the challenges of bereavement. At the same time, in my short introductions to each chapter, I have drawn on my own personal experience to further highlight the immediate relevance of each facet of these teachings to our contemporary lives. Where relevant, I have also described the parallels between the description of the after-death state revealed in *The Tibetan Book of the Dead* with the accounts of near-death experiences documented in contemporary medical research.

As the Dalai Lama discusses in his introduction, which follows, meditative techniques both for developing the ability to focus attention on the processes of one's own mind and senses and for penetrating deeper into the nature of our sensory and mental processes lie at the core of the higher meditative practices of Tibetan Buddhism. At the heart of these meditative skills are the sophisticated practices through which the masters of these meditative traditions simulate the process of the dissolution of consciousness at the moment of death and through which the accomplished meditator can develop a penetrating experiential understanding of the processes of the mind in deep sleep, dreams, and the waking state. These highly refined and polished contemplative skills have been part of the daily practice of generation after generation of great masters for more than two thousand years. Still today, when deepening their understanding of the processes of consciousness, it is not unusual for accomplished practitioners to remain in solitary retreat for sustained periods of up to thirty years.

It is the disciplined application of these meditative practices that is the source of the insights presented in this cycle of texts. Within a literary context, we now know that the ultimate source of the insights presented in *The Tibetan Book of the Dead* was first described in the root text on which *The Tibetan Book of the Dead* is based, the *Guhyagarbha Tantra*. This root text is thought to have been originally composed in the sixth century by the Buddhist masters King Indrabhūti and Kukkurāja from Sahor in northwest India. The tantra text itself describes its source as a revelation received by the king, while in retreat, from the primordial buddha Samantabhadra. According to this lineage of Tibetan Buddhism, Samantabhadra is the meditational deity who is the embodiment of pure awareness, the natural purity of mental consciousness. In other words, the text attributes the ultimate source of these teachings to a direct, complete, and sustained experiential understanding of the ultimate nature of mind. A form of meditation, which is still commonly practiced today, for beginning to develop such a sustained experiential understanding is presented in the chapter "Uncovering the Nature of Mind."

The arrival in Tibet of the complete cycle of teachings now known in the West as *The Tibetan Book of the Dead* is attributed in our text to the great Indian Buddhist tantric master Padmasambhava. Padmasambhava, along with the eminent Indian scholar from Nalanda University, Śāntarakṣita, and the Tibetan king Trisong Detsen, formally established Buddhism in Tibet during the eighth century. Most Tibetans today still revere Padmasambhava as "a second Buddha." In other words, he is regarded as one who, through the training of the mind in the various levels of meditative practice, has awoken to a complete knowledge of the mind's actual nature. The mystical story of the first teaching of our text in the court of King Trisong Detsen is described in the histories written by later holders of this lineage of teaching:

When Padmasambhava was nearing the completion of his direct spiritual work and teaching in Tibet, the sovereign, Trisong Detsen, and his son Prince Mutri Tsenpo, along with the translator Chokrolui Gyelsten and others, offered him a maṇḍala of gold and turquoise, and fervently made the following supplication: "Although your compassion is always present and in the past you have held high the incalculable beacons of the teaching, according to the outer and inner vehicles, yet for the benefit of ourselves, the king, ministers, friends, and subjects, and for future beings of the degenerate age, we request you to give a teaching which is the quintessence of all the teachings of the outer and inner vehicles; one through which buddhahood may be attained in a single lifetime; one which will bestow liberation by merely hearing it, a profound and concise teaching containing the essential meaning."

Thus, in response to their supplication, the Great Master replied, "O! Sovereign King, Prince, Ministers, in accord with your wish, I do have a teaching which is the essential point of all the six million four hundred thousand tantras of the Great Perfection, which were brought forth from the enlightened intention of glorious Samantabhadra. By merely hearing this teaching, the doors leading to birth in inferior existences will be blocked. By merely understanding it you will arrive at the level of supreme bliss. Those who take its meaning to heart will reach the irreversible level of the spontaneously accomplished awareness holders. It can bring great benefit for all those who are connected with it."

The histories then describe how, after completing the teaching, Padmasambhava requested that it be written down, in a secret script, and buried in the form of a "treasure text" at the sacred Mount Gampodar in Dakpo, southern Tibet, predicting that the text would be discovered at a time suitable for its wider dissemination. Six centuries later, the histories recount, the text was unearthed by the Tibetan master from Dakpo, Karma Lingpa, who some say was a reincarnation of the eighth-century translator Chokrolui Gyelsten. Karma Lingpa's own life history is surprisingly obscure. It is thought, though, that he may have discovered the hidden texts while still in his mid-teens and then passed away at a young age, but, before his untimely death, he did successfully pass the entire corpus of teachings to his son (and possibly to his father too). Initially, following Padmasambhava's directions, the teaching was still then not widely disseminated. It was not until the fifteenth century, when the teachings were received by the third-generation lineage holder Gyarawa Namka Chokyi Gyatso, that its public teaching began and its fame slowly spread throughout the Tibetan Buddhist regions of Asia.[1]

As I have mentioned, awareness of our text in the West began in 1927, when Lama Kazi Dawa Samdup and W. Y. Evans-Wentz's pioneering first translation of three chapters of the complete work first appeared. It was Evans-Wentz who coined the title *The Tibetan Book of the Dead* for his edition, a title that has been retained in all subsequent translations and related studies. Immediately upon its first publication, the text's detailed description of the after-death state and its sophisticated psychological insights caused a considerable stir among influential intellectual and literary circles of Europe and North America. In his psychological commentary, published with Evans-Wentz's edition, the eminent Swiss psychiatrist and founder of analytical psychology, Carl Jung, wrote:

> [*The Tibetan Book of the Dead*] belongs to that class of writings [which], because of their deep humanity and their still deeper insight into the secrets of the human psyche, make an especial appeal to the layman who is seeking to broaden

KARMA LINGPA

his knowledge of life. For years, ever since it was first published, the *Bardo Thödol* [*The Tibetan Book of the Dead*] has been my constant companion, and to it I owe not only many stimulating ideas and discoveries, but also many fundamental insights.

In the 1960s, with the arrival of American counterculture, the experimentation with hallucinogens, and the often playful enthusiasm for exploring the boundaries of human experience, came Timothy Leary's *The Psychedelic Experience*, an interpretation of Evans-Wentz's translation from a psychedelic perspective. Evans-Wentz's edition then rearose as something of a counterculture classic, spurred on by the interests of such literary icons of the time as William Burroughs, Allen Ginsberg, and Jack Kerouac.

Sadly though, beginning in the late 1950s, the tragedy of the military invasion of Tibet by China's Red Army forced many of Tibet's greatest twentieth-century masters to seek sanctuary in India and other countries. Paradoxically, even though China's military takeover and the consequent cultural revolution profoundly disrupted Tibet's living Buddhist heritage, for the first time Western Buddhist scholars were now able to study directly with Tibet's great masters. Resettled in India and Nepal, many of the great teachers who, before the Chinese occupation, had completed their studies and had often concluded long periods of solitary retreat, worked enthusiastically with their foreign students on the preparation of new translations. Gradually the accumulated knowledge of more than two thousand years of disciplined investigation into the nature of human experience began to be authentically translated. A vast treasury of new insights across many of the major facets of human inquiry began to be uncovered and the astonishing sophistication, scope, and depth of Tibetan Buddhist culture gradually became more widely known.

Today, this translation work is continuing in universities and study centers around the world. There is still much to do! Even in relation to our text, the compendium of twelve chapters that comprises *The Tibetan Book of the Dead* is in fact part of a greater cycle of teachings which extends to more than sixty-five individual texts. Some scholars estimate that even now, after forty years of continuous translation activity, less than 4 percent of Tibet's literary heritage has become available in English. Yet, more and more, we are beginning to see a growing convergence of perspectives between the underlying understandings drawn from the meditative investigation into the nature of mind and the emerging scientific understandings related to the nature of perception, consciousness, and human psychology. Similarly, contemporary medical research into the nature of near-death experiences is mirroring the insights drawn from a long history of meditative investigation into the subtler levels of consciousness.

At the heart of the Buddhist investigation into the nature of our experience are the collected insights of individuals who, from ancient times until today, have followed the meditative techniques taught by their masters and who have arrived at a depth of understanding that concurs with that of their peers and with that of the past generations of teachers. Although it is very hard to accomplish this depth of understanding without intense dedication and without a teacher, we can all reflect on the experiences of the great masters as set down in texts such as ours and, as the great Buddhist teachers of the past have always encouraged us to do, check whether or not our experience concurs with their experience.

I hope in some small way that the extracts presented here will provide an inspiration for such a journey of discovery and dearly wish also that, as the Dalai Lama says in the conclusion to his introductory commentary on our first complete translation of *The Tibetan Book of the Dead*: "I hope that the profound insights contained in this work will be a source of inspiration and support to many interested people around the world."

GRAHAM COLEMAN
2007, Sarnath, India

Introductory Commentary

by His Holiness the XIVth Dalai Lama
Exploring the Notion of Continuity of Consciousness

The question of whether or not there exists a continuity of consciousness after death has been an important aspect of philosophical reflection and debate from ancient Indian times to the present. When considering these matters from a Buddhist point of view, however, we have to bear in mind that the understanding of the nature of continuity of consciousness and the understanding of the nature of the "I" or "self" are closely interlinked. Therefore, let us first look at what it is that can be said to constitute a person.

According to Buddhist classical literature, a person can be seen as possessing five interrelated aggregates, technically known as the five psycho-physical aggregates.[2] These are the aggregate of consciousness, the aggregate of form (which includes our physical body and senses), the aggregate of feeling, the aggregate of discrimination, and the aggregate of motivational tendencies. That is to say, there is our body, the physical world and our five senses, and there

ŚĀKYAMUNI BUDDHA

are the various processes of mental activity, our motivational tendencies, our labeling of and discrimination between objects, our feelings, and the underlying awareness or consciousness.

Among the ancient schools of thought, which accepted the notion of continuity of consciousness, there were several non-Buddhist philosophical schools that regarded the entity, the "I" or "self," which migrated from existence to existence, as being unitary and permanent. They also suggested that this "self" was autonomous in its relationship to the psycho-physical components that constitute a person. In other words they believed or posited that there is an essence or "soul" of the person, which exists independently from the body and the mind of the person.

However, Buddhist philosophy does not accept the existence of such an independent, autonomous entity. In the Buddhist view, the self or the person is understood in terms of a dynamic, interdependent relationship of both mental and physical attributes, that is to say, the psycho-physical components that constitute a person. In other words our sense of self can, upon examination, be seen as a complex flow of mental and physical events, clustered in clearly identifiable patterns—including our physical features, instincts, emotions, and attitudes, etc.—continuing through time. Further, according to Prāsaṅgika-Madhyamaka philosophy, which has become the prevailing philosophical view of Tibetan Buddhism today, this sense of self is simply a mental construct, a mere label given to this cluster of dependently arising mental and physical events in dependence on their continuity.

Now, when we look at this interdependence of mental and physical constituents from the perspective of Highest Yoga

Tantra,[3] there are two concepts of a person. One is the temporary person or self, that is as we exist at the moment, and this is labeled on the basis of our coarse or gross physical body and conditioned mind; and, at the same time, there is a subtle person or self that is designated in dependence on the subtle body and subtle mind. This subtle body and subtle mind are seen as a single entity that has two facets. The aspect that has the quality of awareness, which can reflect and has the power of cognition, is the subtle mind. Simultaneously, there is its energy, the force that activates the mind toward its object—this is the subtle body or vital energy. These two inextricably conjoined qualities are regarded, in Highest Yoga Tantra, as the ultimate nature of a person and are identified as Buddha nature, the essential or actual nature of mind.

Now, before we look more closely at the nature of the subtle body and mind, let us look at how the gross body and mind are thought to originate. The notion of dependent origination lies at the very heart of Buddhist philosophy. The principle of dependent origination asserts that nothing exists in its own right independent of other factors. Things and events come into being only in dependence on the aggregation of multiple causes and conditions. The process through which the external world and the sentient beings within it revolve in a cycle of existence—propelled by karmic propensities and their interaction with misapprehension, attraction and aversion, and conditions—is described in terms of twelve interdependent links. Each cycle of the process begins with a misapprehension of the nature of actual reality. This fundamental ignorance acts as a condition for the arising of the propensities created by our past actions—mental, verbal, and physical—which condition our dualizing consciousness. Our dualizing consciousness, in turn, conditions the qualities and mode of interaction of our psycho-physical aggregates, which condition our sensory fields, which generate contact, which generates sensations, and then in turn attachment, grasping, and maturation toward rebirth. At this point there is an interaction with the genetic constituents of the parents and subsequent interaction with the environment, and then finally we have birth, aging, and death. This cycle can be viewed as both illustrating the underlying processes of life, death, and rebirth and as an illustration of the processes to be transformed on the path to liberation from suffering in cyclic existence.

The notion that there is a connection between this life and the events of both our previous existence and our future existence follows from the Buddhist understanding of the natural law of cause and effect. For example, although we can speak of yesterday's weather and today's weather as distinct, today's weather is inextricably linked with the weather patterns of yesterday. Even at the bodily level, in the case of our physical health for example, we know that events in the past affect the present and those of the present the future. Similarly, in the realm of consciousness the Buddhist view is that there is also this same causal continuum between the events of the past, present, and future.

The Buddhist understanding of the continuity of personal experience, including our memories, can also be considered here. The Buddhist view is that the continuity of personal experience is primarily founded on the capacity for retention, which can be further developed during one's meditative practice in this life. However, generally speaking, it is thought that if a person dies after a prolonged period of illness that has led to a prolonged degeneration of both physical and mental capacities, there will be a greater chance of many of the personal characteristics, including memories, etc., being lost. On the other hand, in the case of someone who dies a sudden death, when the mind-body relationship at the gross level is still very firm, it is thought that there is a greater chance of carrying forward the acquired characteristics and memories, etc. Nonetheless, in both cases, the characteristics carried forward from a previous life are generally thought to be most strongly felt at an early stage of one's rebirth. This is because the personal characteristics of the previous life are thought, generally speaking, to be quickly overwhelmed by the developing characteristics inherited from the parents of the present life. Nonetheless, as I have mentioned, much depends in this respect on the individual's capacity for recall and this capacity for recall is dependent on a deepened retentive training acquired in this lifetime.

Now, let us look at the possible states of existence one can be born into. From the Buddhist perspective, rebirth in conditioned existence can take place in one of three realms: the formless realm, the form realm, or the desire realm. The form and formless realms are fruits of subtle states of consciousness, attained upon the realization of certain meditative concentrations. Our realm, the desire realm, is the most gross of these three. Six classes of beings are described as inhabiting the desire realm: gods (mundane celestial beings whose primary mental state is exaltation), antigods (who are predominantly hostile and jealous), human beings (who are influenced by all the five dissonant mental states), animals (who are under the sway of delusion), anguished spirits (who are under the sway of attachment and unsatisfied craving), and hell beings (who are overwhelmed by hatred, anger, and fear). In the literature of Highest Yoga Tantra, the evolution of all the three realms of conditioned existence is described in terms of differing expressions or states of energy and, as I have mentioned, it is said that our fundamental ignorance is the root of conditioned existence and that karmic energy is its activating force. In the Buddhist view, therefore, it is the nature of our habitual tendencies that generates our future existence, driven by the natural law of cause and effect.

Further, when we observe the patterns of arising and subsiding that underlie the dynamic nature of the physical environment (the cycle of days and nights and the passing of the seasons, for example), and we observe how matter arises from insubstantial subatomic particles, and we look at the patterns of causal connectedness in the arising and dissolution of our mental experiences from moment to moment (across the differing phases of deep sleep, dreams, and our waking state), then the notion of continuity of consciousness can come to be seen to be in accord with both the nature of our environment and the nature of our mental experience. Certainly, it has often been argued that one advantage of accepting the notion of continuity of consciousness is that it gives us a more profound ability to understand and to explain the nature of our existence and of the universe. In addition, this notion of continuity and causal interconnectedness reinforces a sense of consequences for our own actions, in terms of both the impact on ourselves and the impact on others and the environment.

So, in summary, when considering the notion of continuity of consciousness we must bear in mind that there are many different levels of greater or lesser subtlety in the states of consciousness. For example, we know of course that certain qualities of sensory perception are dependent on the physical constitution of the individual and that when the physical body dies, the states of consciousness associated with these sensory perceptions also cease. But, although we know that the human body serves as a condition for human consciousness, the question still remains: what is the nature of the underlying factor or essence that accounts for our experience of consciousness as having the natural quality of luminosity and awareness?

Finally, then, when considering the interrelationship between mind, body, and the environment at the subtle level, we know that material things are composed of cells, atoms, and particles and that consciousness is composed of moments. That is to say that mind and matter have distinctly different natures and therefore have different substantial causes. Material things come into being based on other material entities such as particles, atoms, and cells and the mind comes into being based on a previous moment of mind, which is something that is luminous and has the capacity to be aware. Each moment of awareness therefore depends on a previous moment of awareness as its cause. This is the reasoning upon which Buddhist logic asserts that there is, at the level of subtle mind and subtle wind, a beginningless continuum of mind and matter.

It is through reflection on the above themes—the law of cause and effect, dependent origination, the dynamics of our physical environment, and, based on our analysis of the nature of mind, the mode of the arising and subsiding of thoughts, the shifts in the modalities of our consciousness between deep sleep, dreams, and our waking state, etc.—that the notion of continuity of consciousness may first become established as relevant to the understanding of our current condition. Once the notion of this continuity has been confirmed, through reflection and experience, then it becomes logical to prepare oneself for death and for future existences.

In the literature of Highest Yoga Tantra, as I have mentioned, the three realms of conditioned existence into which a human being may be born are described in terms of differing expressions or modalities of energy (*rlung*), and it is said that our fundamental ignorance is the root of conditioned existence and that karmic energy is its activating force. Further, from the tantric perspective, death, the intermediate state, and rebirth are also seen as nothing other than differing modalities of karmic energy. The point at which the gross levels of energy are completely dissolved—and only the subtle energies remain—is death. The stage at which these energies unfold into a more manifest form is the intermediate state, and the stage at which they eventually manifest substantially is called rebirth. Thus, all three states are differing manifestations of energy (*rlung*). Based on this understanding, since death is the state when all the gross levels of energy and consciousness have been dissolved, and only the subtle energies and consciousnesses remain, it is possible for an advanced yogin to meditatively induce a state that is almost identical to the actual experience of death. This can be achieved because it is possible to meditatively bring about the dissolution of the gross levels of energy and consciousness. When such a task is accomplished, the meditator gains an enormous potential to progress definitively in his or her spiritual practice.

Normally in our lives, if we know that we are going to be confronted by a difficult or unfamiliar situation, we prepare and train ourselves for such a circumstance in advance, so that when the event actually happens we are fully prepared. The rehearsal of the processes of death, and those of the intermediate state, and the emergence into a future existence, lies at the very heart of the path in Highest Yoga Tantra. These practices are part of my daily practice also, and because of this I somehow feel a sense of excitement when I think about the experience of death. At the same time, though, sometimes I do wonder whether or not I will really be able to fully utilize my own preparatory practices when the actual moment of death comes!

LIVING

SONG OF IMPERMANENCE

The sense of sadness, emptiness, and meaninglessness that we experience at the loss of a loved one is one of the most challenging emotions that we encounter in our lives.

I remember vividly the shock and confusion in my own family when my sister's husband died in a road accident, just shortly after their marriage. My family was not on the whole religious and had not considered or prepared for the inevitability of death. Everyone tried to be consoling and to carry on as best they could. But, in the more intimate moments, there were many questions: what is death exactly, how should we behave, how can we help him, can he still see us, if we speak with him, will he hear us . . . ?

At the time of my brother-in-law's death, I was in my early twenties. I had read the abridged 1927 version of *The Tibetan Book of the Dead*, accounts from classical Greece relating to the after-death state, and modern research on near-death experiences, and had begun a lifelong study of Tibetan Buddhism. But it was living in Tibetan communities from my midtwenties onward and later marrying into a Bhutanese family that demonstrated to me so powerfully the freedom and creativity that the Tibetan Buddhist appreciation of death and dying can bring to our everyday life, to our perspective on death, and to coping with bereavement.

My experience of death in my wife's family was very different from that in my own family. There was, of course, profound sadness. But this was tempered by an open acceptance of death as a natural process and the sorrow was creatively transformed by a resolute purposefulness in wishing to do all that was possible to support and comfort my mother-in-law, a mother of seven children, who had passed away.

We know from our everyday lives that our existence is fragile and that every aspect of the world in which we live changes from moment to moment. Usually, though, we do find it very hard to actually accept change or further still to think of change as a source of inspiration. Living close to the rhythms of nature, surrounded by the naked power of the elements, can in itself inspire an appreciation of the fundamental impermanence of all things. Yet in Himalayan cultures, this appreciation also resounds throughout the monastic and lay literatures and throughout the arts. From an early age, children hear songs and poetry describing our journey through life as like "honey on a razor's edge" or "as fragile as a bubble in water." The reality of death is not hidden away, and this acceptance of death as a natural part of life removes so much of the suffering that our clinging to this one physical dimension of our existence generates.

This first extract from the complete *Tibetan Book of the Dead* is a poem that forms part of the daily preliminary practices followed in the monasteries and households of the practitioners of this cycle of teachings. It is beautifully written and flows melodically in Tibetan, and very often one of the first sounds I would hear, on waking in a Bhutanese monastery, was the gentle singing of this poem by the young monks as they swept the courtyard outside my window and prepared to begin their day.

O, Alas! Alas! Fortunate Child of Buddha Nature,
Do not be oppressed by the forces of ignorance and delusion!
But rise up now with resolve and courage!
Entranced by ignorance, from beginningless time until now,
You have had more than enough time to sleep.

So do not slumber any longer, but strive after virtue with
body, speech, and mind!

Are you oblivious to the sufferings of birth, old age, sickness,
and death?

There is no guarantee that you will survive, even past this
very day!

The time has come for you to develop perseverance in your
practice.

For, at this singular opportunity, you could attain the ever-
lasting bliss of nirvāṇa.

So now is certainly not the time to sit idly,

But, starting with the reflection on death, you should bring your practice to completion!

The moments of our life are not expendable,

And the possible circumstances of death are beyond imagination.

If you do not achieve an undaunted confident security now,

What point is there in your being alive, O living creature?

All phenomena are ultimately selfless, empty, and free from conceptual elaboration.

In their dynamic they resemble an illusion, mirage, dream, or reflected image,

A celestial city, an echo, a reflection of the moon in water, a bubble, an optical illusion, or an intangible emanation.

You should know that all things of cyclic existence and nirvāṇa

Accord in nature with these ten similes of illusory phenomena.

All phenomena are naturally uncreated.

They neither abide nor cease, neither come nor go.

They are without objective referent, signless, ineffable, and free from thought.

The time has come for this truth to be realized!

We who are fearless and hard-hearted, despite having seen so many sufferings of birth, old age, sickness, and death,

Are wasting our human lives, endowed with freedom and opportunity, on the paths of distraction.

Grant your blessing, so that we may continuously remember impermanence and death!

Since we do not recognize that impermanent things are unreliable,

Still, even now, we remain attached, clinging to this cycle of existence.

Wishing for happiness, we pass our human lives in suffering.

Grant your blessing, so that attachment to cyclic existence may be reversed!

Our impermanent environment will be destroyed by fire and water,

The impermanent sentient beings within it will endure the severing of body and mind.

The seasons of the year: summer, winter, autumn, and spring, themselves exemplify impermanence.

Grant your blessing, so that disillusionment with conditioned existence may arise from the depths of our hearts!

Last year, this year, the waxing and waning moons,

The days, nights, and indivisible time moments are all impermanent.

If we reflect carefully, we too are face to face with death.

Grant your blessing, so that we may become resolute in our practice!

Though this body endowed with freedom and opportunity is extremely hard to find,

When the Lord of Death approaches in the semblance of disease,

How needing of compassion are those who, bereft of the sacred teachings,

Return empty-handed from this life!

Grant your blessing so that a recognition of urgency may grow in our minds!

Alas! Alas! O Precious Jewel, embodiment of compassion!

Since you, the Conqueror, are endowed with a loving heart,

Grant your blessing, so that we and the six classes of beings

May be liberated, right now, from the sufferings of cyclic existence!

IMPRISONED BY THE EGO: A LAMENT

If we reflect on the way we react to the events in our lives, we can see that it is our own expectations that determine our sense of fulfillment or sorrow from moment to moment. Even if we are just drinking a cup of tea, we expect the tea to be a comfortable temperature as it reaches our lips and are surprised if, for a reason we did not expect, it is too hot and burns us. This pain is not of course the fault of the tea, it is our own—for not knowing that the tea was too hot!

If we look at the nature of our experience, we can see that our expectations are built up around our liking for some things (our hopes, passions, and attachments), or our dislike for others (our fears, hatreds, or aversions), or our sense of pride (our feeling of how we would like others to see us), or our ambition (whatever it is we are trying to achieve at that moment). Even if we are just trying to hammer a nail into a piece of wood, we have the hope that the nail will sit flush with the surface of the wood, we fear that the nail might bend or that we will hit our finger, and we may well be distracted by thoughts of the blow to our pride should we fail altogether. At the heart of our attempt to be successful is whether or not our expectations are realistic. If the wood is too hard or the nail too weak, we will not succeed however hard we try.

In the Buddhist view, determining the way in which our personal experience is generated, from moment to moment, is a primary pursuit. If through our own exploration we come to an understanding that our happiness and sorrow are determined by ourselves, by our own way of reacting to the events of our lives, an extraordinary creative potential is unleashed.

We can begin to loosen the mesmerizing web of the ego's unrealistic expectations—its clouds of hopes, fears, and misunderstandings—and to break through the wall of our separateness from the actual nature of things.

Looking at our own lives, we can see that our expectations are built up from our past experiences, including the consequences of what we have thought, what we have said, and what we have done. In the Buddhist view, it is this stream of evolving experience continuing through time, even from lifetime to lifetime, which determines our entire perceptual realm. Our past experiences are seen as not just shaping our own character but also the nature of the world in which we live. Our happiness and sorrow are seen as dependent on our mental habits built up over many lives. The extent of our lack of recognition of the actual nature of things, the extent of our attachments, our aversions, and the nature of our ambitions—all these collectively determine our entire perceptual realm. Thus, recognizing the role that the ego plays in creating and sustaining this perceptual realm is the key to unlocking our imprisonment created by our past discordant mental habits.

Through the poignant poem that follows, the monks and nuns, as part of their daily practice, appeal to the meditational deity Vajrasattva for inspiration in seeking release from the matrix of heartless imprisonment built by the ego. Vajrasattva is an aspect of the fully enlightened mind, the buddha especially related to purification—that is, with the insight and compassion that removes the dissonance generated by ego-bound thought patterns, speech, and activities.

O<small>M</small> *O great compassionate and transcendent Lord Vajrasattva,*

Whose supremely exquisite form, immaculate and white,

Is suffused by a pure inner radiance, glowing like a hundred thousand suns and moons,

Emanating heroic rays of light, which illuminate the chiliocosm,

You who are known as the guide and teacher of the three levels of existence,

The unique friend to all living beings of the three world-systems,

O Lord of Loving Kindness, deity of compassion, please attend to us!

From beginningless time, without end, I have roamed throughout cyclic existence—

Led astray by the momentum of my mistaken past actions and improper past behavior,

I have mistaken the path and become lost on the path.

I regret with powerful remorse the negative past actions I have committed, of any kind.

Drawn by the momentum of momentary yet violently resonant past acts,

I have sunk into this ocean of suffering, the sea of cyclic existence.

The fires of blazing hatred have unabatingly seared my mind,

The dense darkness of delusion has blinded my discriminative awareness,

The ocean coasts of desire have drowned my consciousness,

The mountain of fierce pride has entombed me in the lower existences,

The cruel whirlwind of envy has sucked me into these turning worlds,

Where, entwined by the tight knot of egocentricity,

I have fallen into the pit of desire, this chasm of blazing fires.

Unbearably brutal misery has poured down on me like heavy rain.

Damaged by such extreme and unbearable suffering,

Seared by the blazing ferocious fires of my negative past actions,

The shoots of my consciousness and sense faculties have been blunted.

If my body, this illusory aggregate, can no longer withstand all this pain,

How can you bear to witness this, O Compassionate Lord of Loving Kindness?

Obscured fool that I am, burdened by the most negative, evil past acts,

Propelled by the momentum of these past actions,

I have taken birth as the personification of rampant egohood within this world-system of desire.

I regret having taken such birth, and am dismayed by my past acts!

Yet, regardless of my regret and my dismay, past actions cannot be remade.

The momentum of past actions is as strong as a river's inexorable flow,

So how can the mighty river of past actions be reversed in a mere moment!

All that ripens is born from one's own past actions,

And I am one who has been swept along by the violent whirlwind of my past actions,

And accordingly have roamed over countless past aeons,

Lost within the dark prisons of cyclic existence.

O Lord of Loving Kindness, through the blessing of your compassion,

Purify the obscurations generated by my past actions and dissonant mental states,

And secure me in the presence of your mother-like loving kindness!

Here am I, continuously yearning for the sight of your compassionate face,
Which shines with a luminosity like that of the sun,
And radiates with a clarity like that of the moon.
Yet my darkened eyes, blinded by the cataracts of beginningless ignorance,
Are unable to see you,
O Lord of Living Beings, where are you now?

When I am terrified by the utterly unbearable and virulent power of past actions,
And my hair stands on end, out of fear,
I call out this lament, in heartfelt passion,
And cry out to you in a voice of utter despair!
O Lord of Loving Kindness, if you do not attend to me with compassion now,
At the time of my death, when my mind and body separate,
When I am cut off from the company of spiritual friends, and dragged away by Yama,
At that time, when my relatives stay behind in the world,
Yet I alone am led away by the power of past actions,
At that time, I will be unprotected and without a refuge.
So, do not on any account hesitate or delay now,
But draw near to me at this very moment,
And enact the wrathful "rites of liberation."

Beings such as I, who are afflicted by past actions,

Have been subject to misconceptions since beginningless time.

As a result, we have not achieved release from the turning states of cyclic existence.

Indeed, beings such as I have assumed such a countless number of corporeal forms,

During countless births in countless aeons,

That if our flesh and bones were to be collected together,

Their accumulated mass would fill this world,

And if our pus and blood were to be collected together,

Their accumulated mass would fill a vast ocean,

And if the residue of our past actions were to be collected together,

Their extent would be beyond conception and inexpressible.

Though I have continued endlessly in a cycle of births and deaths,

Throughout the three world-systems,

The actions that I have committed have been pointless and unproductive.

Yet from among all these many countless births,

The actions committed in the course of just a single lifetime

Could have been worthwhile if only I had trained well,

Pursued the path of unsurpassed enlightenment,

And thus attained the genuine final nirvāṇa.

But, swayed by the virulence of past actions and the great potency of dissonant mental states,

I have assumed bodies, these networks of flesh and blood, and roamed throughout cyclic existence,

Thrust into a succession of prison-like existences,

Where the suffering is hard to bear.

*All my transgressions, resonant with such unbearably in-
tense suffering,*

Have been born out of my own past actions.

*Please, through your great compassion, shatter the momen-
tum of these past actions,*

*And reverse the vital energy of past actions generated by
dissonant mental states!*

*From your heart, O compassionate conquering deity, gaze
upon me now!*

Draw me up from the swamp of cyclic existence!

*Lead me swiftly to the supreme level of the three buddha-
bodies.*

LIVING, DREAMING, MEDITATING, AND DYING

In Tibetan Buddhist cultures, the array of our experiences in our dreams, in our waking state, and in death is seen as inextricably bound together by an underlying continuity. Just as the cycles of day and night are a mere consequence of a turning world, life and death are seen as two facets of the continuity of our awareness.

We know from our own experience that our consciousness expresses itself in different modalities. We know that when we dream the mind can create whole worlds where we can speak, act, see, hear, and touch—just as we do in life. We know also, of course, that while we are awake the mind interacts seamlessly with our physical environment. Also, meditation shows us that in deep sleep, although we do not normally recognize it, the mind dissolves into a subtle nonconceptual state of awareness. This state, which occurs naturally in deep sleep, is very similar to the subtle state of nonconceptual awareness that we can experience in deep meditation while we are awake. This kind of natural shifting between differing modalities of our consciousness—moving back and forth between a subtle nonconceptual state of awareness, as occurs in deep sleep, into a creative dreamlike state, and into our physical waking state—is a normal function of the mind from day to day.

As the Dalai Lama explains in the introductory commentary, these three modalities of consciousness relate closely to the modalities of consciousness at the moment of death, in the intermediate state between death and birth, and in our normal waking state. The point at which both the physical and mental fields of our consciousness dissolve into a naturally radiant, skylike awareness and where both consciousness and energy exist at their most subtle nondual level, as in the subtlest level of deep sleep, we call death. The modality in which both the physical and mental fields of our consciousness arise in a more manifest form—as in a dream, where, although there is perceptual experience, the phenomenal forms are comparatively subtle and nonsubstantive—is the dreamlike intermediate state between death and birth. Then, the modality in which the physical and mental fields of our consciousness assume a gross bodily existence is our normal waking experience between birth and death. Thus, we see a direct parallel between the three natural states of our existence—deep sleep, dreaming, and our waking state—and the three phases of the cycle of living and dying: the moment of death, the intermediate state, and birth.

The higher Tibetan Buddhist teachings also further emphasize the correspondence between the modalities of our consciousness (at the moment of death, in the dreamlike intermediate state, and in our waking state) and the three fields of expression or dimensions of a fully enlightened being. These three dimensions of buddhahood (the dimensions of a being who has fully realized the potential of the mind's nature) are known as buddha-bodies. Here, the fully perfected state of our pure nonconceptual awareness, as in deep sleep, meditation, and the moment of death, is known as the Buddha-body of Reality. The fully perfected state of our dreamlike awareness, as in dreams and in the intermediate state, is known as the Buddha-body of Perfect Resource, and the fully perfected state of our waking state is known as the Buddha-body of Emanation.

In the practices related to *The Tibetan Book of the Dead* (and other Buddhist tantric systems), this direct parallel between the three natural states of our existence and the three dimensions of a fully enlightened being forms the platform for cultivating a fully enlightened state at every phase of our existence: in our normal waking state, while we are dreaming, while we are meditating, and also at the time of death and during the two successive phases of the after-death state.

The short poem that follows, "The Root Verses of the Six Intermediate States," illustrates the nature of our varying modalities of consciousness across the continuity of life and death and reminds the reader of the centrally important practices and perspectives to be adopted at each phase of our journey through time. These verses present a quintessence of the entire *Tibetan Book of the Dead* teachings, and practitioners of this cycle of teachings are encouraged to memorize this poem and to recite it daily, while reflecting on its meaning throughout their lives.

Although these six root verses are succinct and are given here without explanation, the chapters that follow will explore these themes and bring us to a deeper understanding of their practical meaning.

Alas, now as the intermediate state of living arises before me,

Renouncing laziness, for which there is no time in this life,
I must enter the undistracted path of study, reflection, and meditation.

Taking perceptual experience and the nature of mind as the path,
I must cultivate actualization of the three buddha-bodies.
Now, having obtained a precious human body, this one time,
I do not have the luxury of remaining on a distracted path.

Alas, now as the intermediate state of dreams arises before me,

Renouncing the corpse-like, insensitive sleep of delusion,
I must enter, free from distracting memories, the state of the abiding nature of reality.

Cultivating the experience of inner radiance,

Through the recognition, emanation, and transformation of dreams,

I must not sleep like a beast,

But cherish the experiential cultivation which mingles sleep with actual realization.

Alas, now as the intermediate state of meditative concentration arises before me,

Renouncing the mass of distractions and confusions,

I must undistractedly enter a state,

Which is devoid of subjective apprehension, and free from the two extremes,

And attain stability in the stages of generation and perfection.

At this moment, having renounced activity,

And having attained a singular concentration,

I must not fall under the sway of bewildering mental afflictions!

Alas, now as the intermediate state of the time of death arises before me,

Renouncing all attachment, yearning, and subjective apprehension in every respect,

I must undistractedly enter the path, on which the oral teachings are clearly understood,

And eject my own awareness into the uncreated expanse of space.

*Immediately upon separation from this compounded body of
flesh and blood,*

I must know this body to be like a transient illusion.

*Alas, now as the intermediate state of reality arises before
me,*

Renouncing the merest sense of awe, terror, or fear,

*I must recognize all that arises to be awareness, manifesting
naturally of itself.*

*Knowing such sounds, lights, and rays to be visionary phe-
nomena of the intermediate state,*

At this moment, having reached this critical point,

*I must not fear the assembly of Peaceful and Wrathful Dei-
ties, which manifest naturally!*

Alas, now as the intermediate state of rebirth arises before me,

I must with one-pointed intention concentrate my mind,

*And resolutely connect with the residual potency of my vir-
tuous past actions.*

*I must obstruct the womb entrance and call to mind the
methods of reversal.*

*This is the time when perseverance and purity of perception
are imperative.*

*I must give up all jealousy and meditate on my spiritual
teacher with consort.*

This completes the "Root Verses of the Six Intermediate
States."

UNCOVERING THE NATURE
OF MIND

If indeed our waking state, our dream state, and our experiences at the time of death (and during the after-death state) are all facets of an underlying continuity of awareness, what exactly is the nature of this awareness and how can it be uncovered?

The text that follows forms part of a guide that practitioners of *The Tibetan Book of the Dead* teachings take with them on solitary retreats aimed at developing their understanding of the underlying nature of awareness. Before the retreat begins, the spiritual master always performs an empowerment ritual, through which the seed of realization in the student's mind is awakened by contact with the resonance of the master's meditative accomplishment. The master then also gives a detailed line-by-line elucidation of the meaning of the text and instruction on the meditative techniques to be undertaken. Once in retreat, the student is advised to read this text repeatedly in between periods of three to four hours of unbroken meditation.

Even though I have been fortunate to have received formal empowerments from the Dalai Lama, there is a particular memory that has been an inspiration to me ever since my early twenties.

It was 1977 and I was sitting in the antechamber to His Holiness's residence waiting to be called for an audience. The room was simply decorated, with traditional Tibetan carpets, wooden-framed sofas, and small carved wooden tables. A cup of tea, which the Dalai Lama's attendant had brought for me, was steaming softly in a shaft of sunlight shining through glass doors that led into the courtyard where His Holiness gives his public audiences. From time to time I could hear the Dalai Lama's voice echoing through the wall from his private chamber and I was looking out across the courtyard at the peaceful gardens and sun-bathed, towering mountains beyond. I had been privileged to have seen the Dalai Lama quite often during this time and I was sitting contentedly, peacefully gazing out through the glass doorway without any special thoughts or expectations. From time to time an attendant monk to the Dalai Lama walked across the courtyard and his robe would brush against the flowers and bushes surrounding the paved courtyard, sending shudders of disturbance trembling along the borders. Gradually, my normal conceptual appreciation of my perceptual experience began to dissolve. I could still see, hear, and smell clearly, but there was an extraordinary sense of perfection and completeness in every facet of what I saw, thought, and felt. Everything was clearly identifiable as it was. I felt neither drawn to nor separate from all that surrounded me and absolutely engaged with and fulfilled by every instant of my moment-by-moment experience. It was as if all the conditioned habits of my normal way of seeing had suddenly vanished and I was experiencing the naked freshness of my own mind and perceptions for the first time. There was both the sensory image and a completely spacious pure awareness present and indivisibly mingled at the same time. It was as if everything had been turned inside out. I no longer felt that I was perceiving a fixed, physical world alien from myself, but that my entire perceptual realm was bound together by a deeply peaceful, benign vitality and warmth. The feeling of well-being that arose and the sense of open, alert spaciousness that accompanied each moment of experience were exquisitely indescribable. It was as if my own awareness and my perceptual field had joined together for the first time, like two parts of a broken vase, and turned back into the form they had always supposed to be.

Although I never mentioned this experience to His Holiness, I did of course feel that this glimpse of a transformed way of being had been inspired by him. This first introduction to a purer form of awareness, beyond my normal conceptual states, was the first and most potent revelation of a more exalted awareness that I have experienced in my life and is one of my most cherished memories. It was of course an all-too-transitory taste of a quality of being that I had never experienced so vividly before, and it was by no means any kind of meditative accomplishment on my part, but it was an introduction that pointed the way, just as the text presented in this chapter is intended to do.

Taking as its starting point the exploration of the space between our thoughts, the focus of the text that follows is the discovery of the ultimate nature of one's own mind by looking into one's own mind without any conceptual interpretation. This text forms part of one of the most direct and highly revered systems of meditation in the Tibetan tradition, known as "The Great Perfection" or "Dzogchen," and is titled "The Introduction to Awareness: Natural Liberation Through Naked Perception."

Though the single nature of mind, which completely pervades both cyclic existence and nirvāṇa,

Has been naturally present from the beginning, you have not recognized it.

Even though its radiance and awareness have never been interrupted,

You have not yet encountered its true face.

Even though it arises unimpededly in every facet of existence,

You have not as yet recognized this single nature of mind.

In order that this single nature might be recognized by you,

The conquerors of the three times have taught an inconceivably vast number of practices,

Including the eighty-four thousand aspects of the sacred teachings.

*Yet despite this diversity, not even one of these teachings has
been given by the conquerors,*

Outside the context of an understanding of this nature!

*And even though there are inestimable volumes of sacred
writings, equally vast as the limits of space,*

*Actually, these teachings can be succinctly expressed in a few
words, which are the introduction to awareness.*

*The following is the introduction to the means of experienc-
ing this single nature of mind*

Through the application of three considerations:

*First, recognize that past thoughts are traceless, clear, and
empty,*

*Second, recognize that future thoughts are unproduced and
fresh,*

*And third, recognize that the present moment abides natu-
rally and unconstructed.*

*When this ordinary, momentary consciousness is examined
nakedly and directly by oneself,*

Upon examination, it is a radiant awareness,

Which is free from the presence of an observer,

Manifestly stark and clear,

Completely empty and uncreated in all respects,

Lucid, without duality of radiance and emptiness,

*Not permanent, for it is lacking inherent existence in all
respects,*

Not a mere nothingness, for it is radiant and clear,

*Not a single entity, for it is clearly perceptible as a multiplic-
ity,*

*Yet not existing inherently as a multiplicity, for it is indi-
visible and of a single savor.*

*This intrinsic awareness, which is not extraneously de-
rived,*

*Is itself the genuine introduction to the abiding nature of all
things.*

*When the introduction is powerfully applied in accordance
with the above method for entering into this reality:*

One's own immediate consciousness is this very reality!

*Abiding in this reality, which is uncontrived and naturally
radiant,*

*How can one say that one does not understand the nature of
mind?*

*Abiding in this reality, wherein there is nothing on which to
meditate,*

*How can one say that, by having entered into meditation,
one was not successful?*

*Abiding in this reality, which is one's actual awareness
itself,*

How can one say that one could not find one's own mind?

*Abiding in this reality, the uninterrupted union of radiance
and awareness,*

*How can one say that the true face of mind has not been
seen?*

Abiding in this reality, which is itself the cognizer,

How can one say that, though sought, this cognizer could not be found?

Abiding in this reality, where there is nothing at all to be done,

How can one say that, whatever one did, one did not succeed?

Given that it is sufficient to leave this awareness as it is, uncontrived,

How can one say that one could not continue to abide in that state?

Given that it is sufficient to leave it as it is, without doing anything whatsoever,

How can one say that one could not do just that?

Given that, within this reality, radiance, awareness, and emptiness are inseparable and spontaneously present,

How can one say that, by having practiced, one attained nothing?

Given that this reality is naturally originating and spontaneously present, without causes or conditions,

How can one say that, by having made the effort to find it, one was incapable of success?

Given that the arising and liberation of conceptual thoughts occur simultaneously,

How can one say that, by having applied this antidote to conceptual thoughts, one was not effective?

Abiding in this immediate consciousness itself,

How can one say that one does not know this reality?

Be certain that the nature of mind is empty and without foundation.

One's own mind is insubstantial, like an empty sky.

Look at your own mind to see whether it is like that or not.

Divorced from views which constructedly determine the nature of emptiness,

Be certain that pristine cognition, naturally originating, is primordially radiant—

Just like the nucleus of the sun, which is itself naturally originating.

Look at your own mind to see whether it is like that or not!

Be certain that this awareness, which is pristine cognition, is uninterrupted,

Like the coursing central torrent of a river which flows unceasingly.

Look at your own mind to see whether it is like that or not!

Be certain that conceptual thoughts and fleeting memories are not strictly identifiable,

But insubstantial in their motion, like the breezes of the atmosphere.

Look at your own mind to see whether it is like that or not!

Be certain that all that appears is naturally manifest in the mind,

Like the images in a mirror which also appear naturally.

Look at your own mind to see whether it is like that or not!

Be certain that all characteristics are liberated right where they are,

Like the clouds of the atmosphere, naturally originating and naturally dissolving.

Look at your own mind to see whether it is like that or not!

There are no phenomena extraneous to those that originate from the mind.

So, how could there be anything on which to meditate apart from the mind?

There are no phenomena extraneous to those that originate from the mind.

So, there are no modes of conduct to be undertaken extraneous to those that originate from the mind.

There are no phenomena extraneous to those that originate from the mind.

So, there are no commitments to be kept extraneous to those that originate from the mind.

There are no phenomena extraneous to those that originate from the mind.

So, there are no results to be attained extraneous to those that originate from the mind.

There are no phenomena extraneous to those that originate from the mind.

So, one should observe one's own mind, looking into its nature again and again.

If, upon looking outward toward the external expanse of the sky,

There are no projections emanated by the mind,

And if, on looking inward at one's own mind,

There is no projectionist who projects thoughts by thinking them,

Then, one's own mind, completely free from conceptual projections, will become luminously clear.

This intrinsic awareness, union of inner radiance and emptiness, is the Buddha-body of Reality,

Appearing like the illumining effect of a sunrise on a clear and cloudless sky,

It is clearly knowable, despite its lack of specific shape or form.

There is a great distinction between those who understand and those who misunderstand this point.

This naturally originating inner radiance, uncreated from the very beginning,

Is the parentless child of awareness—how amazing!

It is the naturally originating pristine cognition, uncreated by anyone—how amazing!

This radiant awareness has never been born and will never die—how amazing!

Though manifestly radiant, it lacks an extraneous perceiver— how amazing!

Though it has roamed throughout cyclic existence, it does not degenerate—how amazing!

Though it has seen buddhahood itself, it does not improve—how amazing!

Though it is present in everyone, it remains unrecognized—how amazing!

Still, one hopes for some attainment other than this—how amazing!

Though it is present within oneself, one continues to seek it elsewhere—how amazing!

Now follows the esoteric instruction which reveals the three times to be one:

Abandon your notions of the past, without attributing a temporal sequence!

Cut off your mental associations regarding the future, without anticipation!

Rest in a spacious modality, without clinging to the thoughts of the present.

Do not meditate at all, since there is nothing upon which to meditate.

Instead, revelation will come through undistracted mindfulness—

Since there is nothing by which you can be distracted.

Nakedly observe all that arises in this modality, which is without meditation and without distraction!

When this experience arises,

Intrinsically aware, naturally cognizant, naturally radiant and clear,

It is called "the mind of enlightenment."

Since within this mind of enlightenment there is nothing upon which to meditate,

This modality transcends all objects of knowledge.

Since within this mind of enlightenment there are no distractions,

It is the radiance of the essence itself.

This Buddha-body of Reality, union of radiance and emptiness,

In which the duality of appearance and emptiness is naturally liberated,

Becomes manifest in this way, unattained by the structured path to buddhahood.

Though one were to scan the entire external universe,

Searching for the nature of mind, one would not find it.

Buddhahood cannot be attained other than through the mind.

Not recognizing this, one does indeed search for the mind externally,

Yet how can one find one's own mind when one looks for it elsewhere?

This is like a fool, for example, who, when finding himself amid a crowd of people,

Becomes mesmerized by the spectacle of the crowd and forgets himself,

Then, no longer recognizing who he is, starts searching elsewhere for himself,

Continually mistaking others for himself.

Similarly, since one does not discern the abiding nature,

Which is the fundamental reality of all things,

One is cast into cyclic existence, not knowing that appearances are to be identified with the mind,

And, not discerning one's own mind to be buddha, nirvāṇa becomes obscured.

The apparent dichotomy between cyclic existence and nirvāṇa is due to the dichotomy between ignorance and awareness,

But there is in reality no temporal divide between these two, even by a single moment.

Seeing the mind as extraneous to oneself is indeed bewildering,

Yet bewilderment and nonbewilderment are of a single essence.

Since there exists no intrinsic dichotomy in the mental continuum of sentient beings,

The uncontrived nature of mind is liberated just by being left in its natural state.

Yet if you remain unaware that bewilderment originates in the mind,

You will never understand the meaning of actual reality.

So you should observe that which naturally arises and naturally originates within your own mind.

First, observe the source from which these appearances initially originated,

Second, observe the place in which they abide in the interim,

And third, observe the place to which they will finally go.

Then, one will find that, just as, for example, a pond-dwelling crow does not stray from its pond,

Even though it flies away from the pond,

Similarly, although appearances arise from the mind,

They arise from the mind and subside into the mind of their own accord.

This nature of mind, which is all-knowing, aware of everything, empty and radiant,

Is established to be the manifestly radiant and self-originating pristine cognition,

Present from the beginning, just like the sky,

As an indivisible union of emptiness and radiance.

This itself is actual reality.

The indication that this is the actual reality is that all phenomenal existence is perceived in the single nature of one's own mind;

And this nature of mind is aware and radiant.

Therefore, recognize this nature to be like the sky!

However, this example of the sky, though used to illustrate actual reality,

Is merely a symbol, a partial and provisional illustration.

For the nature of mind is aware, empty, and radiant in all respects,

While the sky is without awareness, empty, inanimate, and void.

Therefore, the true understanding of the nature of mind is not illustrated by the metaphor of the sky.

To achieve this understanding, let the mind remain in its own state, without distraction!

Now, with regard to the diversity of relative appearances:

They are all perishable; not one of them is genuinely existent.

All phenomenal existence, all the things of cyclic existence and nirvāṇa,

Are the discernible manifestations of the unique essential nature of one's own mind.

This is known because whenever one's own mental continuum undergoes change,

There will arise the discernible manifestation of an external change.

Therefore, all things are the discernible manifestations of mind.

Yet even though all those appearances, of which one is aware in one's own mind,

Do arise as discernible manifestations,

Buddhahood is present simply when they are not subjectively apprehended or grasped.

Bewilderment does not come about on account of these appearances—

But it does come about through their subjective apprehension.

Thus, if the subjectively apprehending thoughts are known

to be of the single nature of mind, they will be liberated of their own accord.

All things that appear are manifestations of mind.

The surrounding environment which appears to be inanimate, that too is mind.

The sentient life-forms which appear as the six classes of living beings, they too are mind.

The joys of both the gods and humans of the higher existences which appear, they too are mind.

The sorrows of the three lower existences which appear, they too are mind.

The five poisons, representing the dissonant mental states of ignorance, which appear, they too are mind.

The awareness, that is self-originating pristine cognition which appears, it too is mind.

The beneficial thoughts conducive to attainment of nirvāṇa which appear, they too are mind.

The obstacles of malevolent forces and spirits which appear, they too are mind.

The deities and spiritual accomplishments which manifest exquisitely, they too are mind.

The diverse kinds of pure vision which appear, they too are mind.

The nonconceptual one-pointed abiding in meditation which appears, it too is mind.

The colors characteristic of objects which appear, they too are mind.

The state without characteristics and without conceptual elaboration which appears, it too is mind.

The nonduality of the single and the multiple which appears, it too is mind.

The unprovability of existence and nonexistence which appears, it too is mind.

There are no appearances at all apart from those that originate in the mind.

The unimpeded nature of mind assumes all manner of appearances.

Yet though these appearances arise, they are without duality,

And they naturally subside into the modality of mind,

Like waves in the waters of an ocean.

Whatever names are given to these unceasingly arising objects of designation,

In actuality, there is but one single nature of mind,

And that single nature of mind is without foundation and without root.

Therefore, it is not perceptible at all, in any direction whatsoever.

It is not perceptible as substance, for it lacks inherent existence in all respects.

It is not perceptible as emptiness, for it is the resonance of awareness and radiance.

It is not perceptible as diversity, for it is the indivisibility of radiance and emptiness.

This present intrinsic awareness is manifestly radiant and clear,

And even though there exists no known means by which it can be fabricated,

And even though this awareness is without inherent existence,

It can be directly experienced.

Thus, if it is experientially cultivated, all beings will be liberated.

All those of all differing potential, regardless of their acumen or dullness,

May realize this intrinsic awareness.

However, for example, even though sesame is the source of oil, and milk of butter,

But there will be no extract if these are unpressed or unchurned,

Similarly, even though all beings actually possess the seed of buddhahood,

Sentient beings will not attain buddhahood without experiential cultivation.

Nonetheless, even a cowherd will attain liberation if he or she engages in experiential cultivation.

For, even though one may not know how to elucidate this state intellectually,

One will through experiential cultivation become manifestly established in it.

One whose mouth has actually tasted molasses

Does not need others to explain its taste.

But even learned scholars who have not realized this single nature of mind will remain the victims of bewilderment.

For however learned and knowledgeable in explaining the nine vehicles they may be,

They will be like those who spread fabulous tales of remote places they have never seen,

And as far as the attainment of buddhahood is concerned,

They will not approach it, even for an instant.

So it is that, for the purpose of nakedly perceiving the manifestly present intrinsic awareness,

This Natural Liberation Through Naked Perception *is most profound.*

Thus, by following this instruction, one should familiarize oneself with this intrinsic awareness.

WISDOMS, ELEMENTS, AND SUBTLE ENERGIES

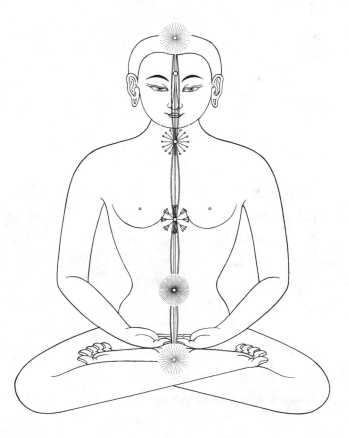

According to the higher teachings of Tibetan Buddhism, the mind and the subtle energies on which the mind rides are the creators of everything we experience. There is nothing that exists separate from our experience of the mind: all phenomena—whether they are our thoughts, emotions, or what we see, hear, or touch—are all experienced through the mind. Therefore the way in which we perceive through the mind is absolutely fundamental to the way we actually experience ourselves and our environment.

Metaphorically speaking, one could describe this understanding of the nature of our personal experience as follows: the ultimate nature of the mind is like a film projector producing a clear, luminous awareness through a clear unclouded film. But, in our ordinary state, it is our own habitual mental constructs that create and shape images on the film, which then appear projected on the screen of our mental awareness—which we then interpret as being real. In other words, everything that we experience is conditioned by our own habitual mental tendencies generated in the past, and what we see and experience as being tangibly real is a projection manufactured by our mental habits and constructs.

This is a truly extraordinary thing to understand—because it gives us a fundamental creative freedom. In the Buddhist view, what we perceive as our external reality is definitely not fixed and what we experience in ourselves is not anybody else's responsibility. By accepting responsibility for our own way of perceiving, we can look into our minds and begin to understand how our own experience comes about—and then we can learn how to transform our experience. This is the very heart of the Buddhist teachings.

The beautiful poem that follows is a blend of two meditations, which would usually be practiced each day by the followers of *The Tibetan Book of the Dead* cycle of teachings. The aim of the meditations is to provide a means by which we can cultivate an unwavering recognition of the underlying natural purity of our own mind, body, and environment.

According to this tradition, the perfected states of our awareness, psycho-physical aggregates, elemental properties, and sensory and mental processes reside at specific points in the subtle energy system of the body. In this practice, the meditational deities, which embody these perfected states, are visualized at the appropriate places within the body. As the meditational deities are visualized, the quality of awareness they embody is experientially cultivated. In this way a recognition of the natural purity of our own impure habitual tendencies is continuously cultivated and a perfected state of being and perception is aroused that encompasses all phenomena.

According to the practitioners of this tradition, a measure of the successful training in this meditation is that the location and nature of the meditational deities will be remembered even in our dreams and that in our waking state there will be an unbroken recognition of the underlying purity of all phenomena, sounds, and thoughts.

Within the expanse of a seminal point, located at the center
of one's heart,
   Is Samantabhadra, the Buddha-body of Reality,
   Father of all buddhas, the natural purity of mental con-
sciousness,
   The primary buddha, unchanging body of light,
   Sky blue, and seated in the posture of meditative equipoise.

   Joyously embracing her consort, in supreme bliss,
   Is Samantabhadrī, the supreme consort,
   Natural purity of the sensory spectrum of phenomena,
   Stainless white, like crystal,
   Mother of all buddhas of past, present, and future.

   In the channel center of one's heart
   Is Vairocana, manifestation of supreme buddha-body,

The natural purity of the aggregate of form,
Pure without renunciation of delusion,
Conch white, holding a wheel and a bell,
Seated on an exalted throne supported by lions,
The resplendent pristine cognition of reality's expanse.

In the eastern channel branch of one's heart
Is Vajrasattva, manifestation of supreme buddha-mind,
The natural purity of the aggregate of consciousness,
Pure without renunciation of aversion,
Azure blue, holding a vajra and a bell,
Seated on an exalted throne supported by elephants,
The resplendent mirror-like pristine cognition.

In the southern channel branch of one's heart
Is Ratnasambhava, manifestation of supreme buddha-attributes,
The natural purity of the aggregate of feeling,
Pure without renunciation of pride,
Golden yellow, holding a jewel and a bell,
Seated on an exalted throne supported by horses,
The resplendent pristine cognition of sameness.

In the western channel branch of one's heart
Is Amitābha, manifestation of supreme buddha-speech,
The natural purity of the aggregate of perceptions,
Pure without renunciation of attachment,
Copper red, holding a lotus and a bell,

Seated on an exalted throne supported by peacocks,
The resplendent pristine cognition of discernment.

In the northern channel branch of one's heart
Is Amoghasiddhi, manifestation of supreme buddha-activities,
The natural purity of the aggregate of motivational tendencies,
Pure without renunciation of envy,
Turquoise green, holding a crossed vajra and a bell,
Seated on an exalted throne supported by cīvaṃcīvaka birds,
The resplendent pristine cognition of accomplishment.

Joyously embracing her consort, in supreme bliss,
In the channel center of one's heart
Is Dhātvīśvarī, the supreme consort,
The mother of the Buddha family, natural purity of space,
Moonlike white, holding a wheel and a bell.

Joyously embracing her consort, in supreme bliss,
In the eastern channel branch of one's heart
Is Buddhalocanā, the supreme consort,
The mother of the Vajra family, natural purity of earth,
Beryl blue, holding a vajra and a bell.

Joyously embracing her consort, in supreme bliss,
In the southern channel branch of one's heart

Is *Māmakī, the supreme consort,*
The mother of the Ratna family, natural purity of water,
Minium orange, holding a jewel and a bell.

Joyously embracing her consort, in supreme bliss,
In the western channel branch of one's heart
Is Pāṇḍaravāsinī, the supreme consort,
The mother of the Padma family, natural purity of fire,
Fire-crystal red, holding a lotus and a bell.

Joyously embracing her consort, in supreme bliss,
In the northern channel branch of one's heart,
Is Samayatārā, the supreme consort,
The mother of the Karma family, natural purity of wind,
Sapphire green, holding a crossed vajra and a bell.

To the right, at the eastern channel branch,
Is Kṣitigarbha, male bodhisattva who acts for the benefit of
beings,
The natural purity of visual consciousness, transcendent of
renunciation,
Snow-mountain white, holding a seedling and a bell.

To the left, at the eastern channel branch,
Is Maitreya, male bodhisattva who acts for the benefit of
beings,
The natural purity of auditory consciousness, transcendent
of renunciation,

Cloud white, holding a blossoming orange bush and a bell.

To the right, at the southern channel branch,
Is Samantabhadra, male bodhisattva who acts for the
benefit of beings,
The natural purity of olfactory consciousness, transcendent
of renunciation,
Amber yellow, holding a grain-sheaf and a bell.

To the left, at the southern channel branch,
Is Ākāśagarbha, male bodhisattva who acts for the benefit
of beings,
The natural purity of gustatory consciousness, transcendent
of renunciation,
Burnished golden-yellow, holding a sword and a bell.

To the right, at the western channel branch,
Is Avalokiteśvara, male bodhisattva who acts for the benefit
of beings,
The natural purity of tactile consciousness, transcendent of
renunciation,
Coral red, holding a lotus and a bell.

To the left, at the western channel branch,
Is Mañjuśrīkumārabhūta, male bodhisattva who acts for
the benefit of beings,
The natural purity of mental consciousness, transcendent of
renunciation,

Minium orange, holding a lily and a bell.

To the right, at the northern channel branch,
Is Nivāraṇaviṣkambhin, male bodhisattva who acts for the
benefit of beings,
The natural purity of the ground-of-all consciousness, tran-
scendent of renunciation,
Green as the night-flowering lotus, holding a book and a bell.

To the left, at the northern channel branch,
Is Vajrapāṇi, male bodhisattva who acts for the benefit of
beings,
The natural purity of deluded consciousness, transcendent of
renunciation,
Emerald green, holding a vajra and a bell.

To the front, at the eastern channel branch,
Is Lāsyā, female bodhisattva whose offerings delight
The eyes of all Those Gone to Bliss, past, present, and future,
The natural purity of visual phenomena, transcendent of
renunciation,
Quartz white, holding a mirror and a bell.

To the rear, at the eastern channel branch,
Is Puṣpā, female bodhisattva whose offerings delight
The minds of all Those Gone to Bliss, past, present, and fu-
ture,

The natural purity of past conceptual thoughts, transcendent
of renunciation,
　Pearl white, holding a white lotus and a bell.

To the front, at the southern channel branch,
　Is Mālyā, female bodhisattva whose gestures delight
　The minds of all Those Gone to Bliss, past, present, and fu-
ture,
　The natural purity of indeterminate conceptual thoughts,
transcendent of renunciation,
　Saffron yellow, holding a garland and a bell.

To the rear, at the southern channel branch,
　Is Dhūpā, female bodhisattva whose offerings delight
　The noses of all Those Gone to Bliss, past, present, and fu-
ture,
　The natural purity of fragrance, transcendent of renuncia-
tion,
　Golden yellow in color, holding sweet-smelling incense and
a censer.

To the front, at the western channel branch,
　Is Gītā, female bodhisattva whose offerings delight
　The ears of all Those Gone to Bliss, past, present, and fu-
ture,
　The natural purity of sound, transcendent of renunciation,
　Marsh mallow pink, and playing a lute.

To the rear, at the western channel branch,
Is Ālokā, female bodhisattva whose offerings delight
The eyes of all Those Gone to Bliss, past, present, and fu-
ture,
The natural purity of future conceptual thoughts, transcen-
dent of renunciation,
Lotus pink, and holding a glowing butter lamp.

To the front, at the northern channel branch,
Is Gandhā, female bodhisattva whose offerings delight
The bodies of all Those Gone to Bliss, past, present, and fu-
ture,
The natural purity of present conceptual thoughts, transcen-
dent of renunciation,
Poppy green, holding a perfume-filled conch.

To the rear, at the northern channel branch,
Is Nartī, female bodhisattva whose offerings delight
The tongues of all Those Gone to Bliss, past, present, and
future,
The natural purity of taste, transcendent of renunciation,
Marine green, holding a deliciously nutritious food of-
fering.

In the channel branch at the eastern gate of one's heart
Is Trailokya-Vijaya, male gatekeeper whose wrathful pres-
ence
Guards against obstacles at the eastern gate,

The natural purity of eternalist views, transcendent of re-
nunciation,
  White, holding a cudgel and a bell.

In the channel branch at the southern gate of one's heart
Is Yamāntaka, male gatekeeper whose wrathful presence
Guards against obstacles at the southern gate,
The natural purity of nihilistic views, transcendent of re-
nunciation,
  Yellow, holding a skull-club and a bell.

In the channel branch at the western gate of one's heart
Is Hayagrīvarāja, male gatekeeper whose wrathful pres-
ence
  Guards against obstacles at the western gate,
The natural purity of egotistical views, transcendent of re-
nunciation,
  Red, holding an iron chain and a bell.

In the channel branch at the northern gate of one's heart
Is Amṛtakuṇḍalin, male gatekeeper whose wrathful pres-
ence
  Guards against obstacles at the northern gate,
The natural purity of substantialist views,⁴ transcendent of
renunciation,
  Green, holding a crossed vajra and a bell.

In the channel branch at the eastern gate of one's heart

Is *Vajrankuśā, female gatekeeper whose immeasurable compassion*
Guides the six classes of beings away from their mundane realms,
White, holding an iron hook that attracts,
She embraces her wrathful consort in blissful union.

In the channel branch at the southern gate of one's heart
Is Vajrapāśā, female gatekeeper whose immeasurable loving kindness
Acts ceaselessly on behalf of beings,
Yellow, holding a noose that lassoes,
She embraces her wrathful consort in blissful union.

In the channel branch at the western gate of one's heart
Is Vajrasphoṭā, female gatekeeper whose immeasurable sympathetic joy
Embraces each and every living being,
Red, holding an iron chain that binds,
She embraces her wrathful consort in blissful union.

In the channel branch at the northern gate of one's heart
Is Vajraghaṇṭā, female gatekeeper whose immeasurable equanimity
Transcends discrimination between living beings.
Green, holding a bell that summons,
She embraces her wrathful consort in blissful union.

DYING

BODY AND MIND DISSOLVING

Modern science tells us that all material phenomena pass to and fro between visible and invisible states. Our physical environment, in its ultimate nature, is a dynamic array of invisible particles whose energy continues through time—only the form changes. Looking into our own minds we can also see that all our thoughts arise from an ineffable, formless spaciousness—they remain present in the mind for a while and then fade away, back into that ineffable state. We know therefore from our own experience that there is a basic pattern of emergence and dissolution that is common to both animate and inanimate phenomena.

In the Buddhist view, this parallel pattern of emergence and dissolution, which we see in both the mind and our physical environment, is to be expected. The mind in its ultimate nature is understood to be a combination of awareness and the subtle energies on which awareness rides. Further, in their gross forms, certain of these subtle energies are related to the qualities of the five elements: space, movement or energy, heat or light, moisture or liquidity, and finally solidity. In turn, these five elemental properties are seen as the underlying components that constitute both our bodies and our physical environment. Hence, according to the Buddhist view, there is a continuum between the formless, the subtly manifest, and the physical—across all phenomena.

This appreciation of the underlying continuity and interdependence between subtle and gross states (both mental and physical) is a cornerstone of the meditational systems presented in the Buddhist tantras. Because the arising and dissolution of our gross states of consciousness is a natural process—they arise from a subtle nonconceptual state and dissolve back into a subtle nonconceptual state—it is possible to induce and observe the arising and dissolution of conceptual states in meditation. Training in this process lies at the core of the higher meditational practices. Initially, the process of the arising and dissolution of our normal conceptual states of mind is rehearsed in visualization, but, as the meditator matures, he or she develops the skill to actually cut off the activity of the gross energies, which serve as a vehicle for our normal conceptual states. Further, since death is the state when all the gross levels of energy and consciousness have dissolved, and only the subtle energies and consciousnesses remain, it is possible for an advanced practitioner to meditatively induce a state almost identical to the actual experience of death. Here the meditator gains the ability to enter into the direct experience of inner radiance, the ultimate underlying nature of mind, and also gains the ability to experience the subtle processes by which conceptual states reemerge from the skylike spaciousness of inner radiance.

Based in part on the insights gained from these meditative techniques, the verses that follow describe the processes of the dissolution of the elemental properties, which support the body, and the dissolution of our conceptual states at the time of death.

At the time of my father's passing away, I had studied and received teachings on several of the major Tibetan Buddhist texts relating to the process of dying and I was privileged to have witnessed the awesome dignity and calm with which accomplished lamas approach the time of their own death. My father was someone who had avoided thinking about death throughout his life. He had always been healthy and as he became ill, in his late seventies, he would often become frustrated and angry with those closest to him. Even though I was scared by the thought of how fearful he might now be, I knew that the last thing he would want to hear was me talking to him about dying. Strangely though, a few weeks before his death, he looked at me very seriously and said: "I have decided to retire now." At the time, I thought he was lost in the memories of his working life as an artist, as he sometimes was. Yet I soon realized that from this day onward he was unusually calm and accepting of all that was happening to him. He had decided to let go and to be open to the processes that were engulfing him. Whenever I was with him, I tried to be tender, open, and lighthearted. He also now had a playfulness about him that I had rarely seen even when I was a child. As I sat with him over the last days of his life, it was a revelation to see the gentle power of the processes of dying unfold and to see his quiet acceptance of the unknown experiences that were overtaking him. Much to my joy, when the final moments came, not struggling with the natural process that had seized him, he passed away peacefully.

Now follows the presentation of the signs of extremely near death:

The five sense faculties dissolve sequentially,

And as a sign of this imminent demise of the sense faculties,

One will be unable to digest food and drink, and one may vomit.

Bodily warmth will diminish, the neck will not support the head,

And one will feel that the head is sinking downward.

Then the five elements will dissolve as follows:

The internal earth element comprises flesh and bone.

As an indication of its dissolution into the external earth element,

The body will grow heavy, and its skin will sag toward the ground,

Whereupon, as an internal sign, one will feel that the body is sinking into the earth.

Because the energy of earth will have dissolved into water,

One will be incapable of supporting one's physical form.

Bodily strength will slip away, and consciousness will become clouded.

The internal water element comprises blood and serum.

As an indication of its dissolution into the external water element,

Saliva and nasal mucus will be secreted,

While the throat and the tongue will become dry.

Because the energy of water will have dissolved into fire,

The warmth of the body will slip away,

And consciousness will oscillate between clarity and dullness.

The internal fire element comprises warmth.

As an indication of its dissolution into the external fire element,

The eyes will roll upward, and one will no longer recognize people.

Because the energy of fire will have dissolved into wind,

The warmth of the body will recede.

The internal wind element comprises breath.

As an indication of its dissolution into the external wind element,

The breath will become wheezy, and the limbs will quiver.

As an internal indication, consciousness will become turbulent,

While miragelike flashing and fleeting visions will arise,

And concurrently all lice and nits will leave the body.

Then, the red "generative essence" derived from one's mother will rise upward,

And the phenomenon called "redness" will occur,

Wherein all appearances are suffused by redness.

At that point, appearances will dissolve into the "subtle mental consciousness of increasing redness,"

And the forty patterns of conceptual thought that originate from attachment will cease.

Then, the white "generative essence" derived from one's father will fall downward,

And the phenomenon called "whiteness" will occur,

Wherein all appearances are suffused by whiteness.

At that point, the "increasing redness" will dissolve into the "subtle mind of attainment,"

And the thirty-three patterns of conceptual thought that originate from aversion will cease.

During this process, each exhalation of breath will become increasingly protracted,

While all the blood of the body will converge in the "life channel,"[5]

And then a single drop of blood will form at the heart center.

In this way, the phenomenon called "blackness" will occur,

Engulfing the suffocating mind in blackness,

And one will experience the sensation of falling into darkness, as if into an abyss.

At that point, "attainment" will dissolve into the "subtle mind of near attainment,"

And the seven patterns of conceptual thought that originate from delusion will cease.

During this process, the mouth will open, and the eyes will roll upward,

Exposing their pale underside.

External appearances will fade, as during the setting of the sun,

And finally the sense faculties, memory, and perceptions will all cease,

Whereupon, all external appearances will be absorbed into blackness.

At that point, the exhaled breath will extend from the body by a cubit,

And all internal appearances will also come to resemble darkness.

Then, the blood in the heart will form two drops,
The head will stoop,
And the exhaled breath will extend from the body by an arrow-length.
Following this, the blood in the center of the heart will form three drops,
And, with HIKA-like gasps, the exhaled breath will extend from the body by a double arm-span.
Then, the external breath will cease, and, engulfed by blackness, one will become unconscious.
Then, the white and red "generative essences" will meet together at the heart,
And, as this occurs, one will swoon into a state of blissfulness.
Thus, consciousness dissolves into inner radiance,
Engendering the experience of the "coemergent delight."
At this point, awareness dissolves into actual reality, at the center of the heart, like the meeting of mother and child.
It is at this time that the inner breath will also cease,
And the vital energy and mind will rest in the central channel.

At this moment, the inner radiance of the ground dawns upon all sentient beings,

And, in the case of a few yogins who have achieved realization,

At this moment, the inner radiance of the path meets the inner radiance of the ground,[6]

Like a meeting of a mother and child,

And thus, now, instantaneously, in an ascending and core-penetrating manner,

These yogins will actualize the uncreated Buddha-body of Reality,

And through the Buddha-bodies of Perfect Resource and Emanation,

They will perform inestimable actions for the sake of all beings.

Thus, the three buddha-bodies will be spontaneously present,

And buddhahood will have been attained.

Because of this, one should understand the significance of obtaining a human body,

And cherish the experiential cultivation of the profound sacred teachings.

For, even though the genuine inner radiance of the ground will always arise at the moment of death,

In the case of all beings who have not already realized the inner radiance of the path,

It will not be recognized.

The past births that one has assumed and left behind are countless and infinite,

And, although the inner radiance has indeed arisen an indescribable number of times,

It has been obscured again and again by the dense fog of co-emergent ignorance,

And thereby, one has come to wander endlessly through cyclic existence.

This is why it is important to achieve such a secure level of realization in this life.

ENTERING THE HORIZON OF LIGHT

In Tibetan Buddhist cultures, our state of mind at the moment of death and our reaction to the experiences that unfold after death are seen as determining the nature of our future existence. Thus, when a loved one dies, less emphasis is placed on one's own sorrow and far greater emphasis is placed on supporting the loved one who is passing through this state of transition.

At the time when Sonam Zangmo, my mother-in-law, passed away, as soon as the doctor felt that the moment of her death was approaching, a revered lama, who lived close to the family, was invited to attend. A great master arriving at the house was itself a rare occasion, and while my father-in-law stayed by his wife's bedside, the seven children made all the preparations for the lama's visit. The moment Lama Tseten arrived, his tenderness and calm pervaded the household. The sense of peaceful purposefulness was so solid it was almost tangible. Straightaway, sitting next to the bed of my mother-in-law and holding her in a gentle

gaze, Lama Tseten completed the preparatory practices and began to guide Sonam Zangmo through the various experiential
states that she was beginning to enter. In the adjoining room, the
attending monks were softly chanting the prayers that accompany
the guidance, and throughout the house the whole family and
relatives were busy preparing offerings to be laid out on the family altar and preparing tea and food for the lama and attending
monks.

As he whispered the guiding instructions to my mother-in-
law, Lama Tseten entered into the states of meditation described
in the guiding text, and in this way he offered a support and anchor for her fragile concentration. He encouraged her, in a soft
melodic voice, to approach the moment of death with a mind filled
with loving kindness and filled with the wish to abide, without
distraction, in the experience of the horizonless radiance that
she was about to enter. Seeing Lama Tseten and my mother-in-
law together, I felt an enormous admiration for him. How wonderful that he was able to offer such comfort at a challenging time
such as this. His understanding of the experiences that my
mother-in-law was passing through, the gentle certainty in his
voice, the palpable calm that he radiated, lifted me as well, just in
the few glimpsed moments that I saw them together, to a restful,
accepting peacefulness. I am sure I will never forget my mother-
in-law's loving gaze as she falteringly, yet so tenderly, looked up at
Lama Tseten from her pillow, with eyes filled with appreciation
for his presence next to her, quietly fearless—gazing with uncon-
ditional love, just as a mother might on the faces of her own children as they slept.

Even now as I remember these moments, I feel deeply moved and privileged to have witnessed the caring for a dying loved one within a culture where there is such an established and accepted knowledge of the dying process and where so much of the pain of separation is soothed by a quiet understanding and a natural sense of knowing how best to support a loved one as they leave this world.

Our still young Western scientific knowledge of the inner processes of dying and the moment of death, although beginning to grow, is still largely based on the insights gained from recent medical research into near-death experiences. In such near-death reports, a common initial experience is usually described as a meeting with an all-pervading, glowing luminosity. Often those who have been resuscitated from near-death states, at the time of entering into this radiant expanse of light, also describe experiencing an extraordinary sense of completeness and contentment and a sense of being enveloped by a loving presence. In the Buddhist view, the moment of death is the moment when the mind returns to its own natural state. All conceptual states are dissolved. We are no longer enthralled by the complex, conflicting mindscape created by our past mental habits. Just as in deep meditation, we experience the actual nature of our own pure awareness, an all-pervading sense of contentment, and the deeply peaceful warmth of boundless compassion. As the texts describe, it is like a son or daughter returning to the arms of their mother after a long separation. Contemporary Tibetan masters, who have commented on the research into near-death experiences, do caution that the reported accounts relate to experiences surrounding the process of dying, close to the moment of death, and not of course to the after-death state. Nonetheless, the reports do show remarkable parallels with the descriptions of the moment of death in *The Tibetan Book of the Dead* and related Tibetan Buddhist literature.

Our text, which follows, comes from the most well-known chapter of *The Tibetan Book of the Dead*, the "Great Liberation by Hearing," and sets out the instructions for the attending lama on the procedure for caring for the dying person and the guidance to be given at the moment of death.

Introduction to Inner Radiance at
the Time of Death

It is best if the root spiritual teacher from whom the dying person personally received guidance can be present. If he or she cannot be present, then a spiritual sibling with identical commitments should be called upon, or if none of these can be present, then a spiritual friend holding the same lineage should attend; or if none of these at all can be present, someone who knows how to read aloud with correct pronunciation and clear diction should recite the introductions many times. Thereby, the dying person will remember that which had formerly been introduced by his or her spiritual teacher, and immediately afterward, being set face to face with the inner radiance of the ground, will undoubtedly attain liberation.

Concerning the time for making this introduction: after respiration has ceased, the vital energy is absorbed into the channel of pristine cognition[7] and the consciousness of the deceased naturally arises as a nonconceptual inner radiance. Later, the vital energy will be reversed and escape into the right and left channels and, as a result, the appearances of the subsequent intermediate state of reality will arise suddenly. Therefore, the introduction to inner radiance at the time of death should be made before the vital energy has escaped into the right and left channels. Generally, the length of time during which the inner breath remains present within the central channel is just about the time taken to eat a meal.

As regards the actual mode of making this introduction, it is best if the consciousness transference is effected at that moment when the respiration is about to cease. If it is not, one should say the following words:

.   .   .

O Child of Buddha Nature, (*call the name of the dying person*), the time has now come for you to seek a path. As soon as your respiration ceases, the luminosity known as "the inner radiance of the first intermediate state," which your spiritual teacher formerly introduced to you, will arise. Immediately your respiration ceases, all phenomena will become empty and utterly naked like space. At the same time, a naked awareness will arise, not extraneous to yourself, but radiant, empty, and without horizon or center. At that moment, you should personally recognize this intrinsic nature and rest in the state of that experience. I too will introduce it to you at that time.[8]

.   .   .

These words should be spoken audibly many times, impressing them on the mind of the dying person until respiration ceases.

Then, when the respiration is on the point of ceasing, one should lay the dying person on the right side, in the posture of the lion, and take the pulse. Once the throbbing of the two carotid arteries has stopped, they should be firmly pressed at their pressure points on the neck.[9] Then the vital energy, having entered the central channel, cannot reverse and escape and it will certainly emerge through the crown fontanelle.[10] The introduction should continue to be made at this time.

This phase in the process of death is called "the inner radiance of reality during the first intermediate state." It is the unique and incontrovertible enlightened intention of the Buddha-body of Reality, which arises in the minds of all living beings. At the moment of death, this coincides with the period when the vital energy is absorbed into the central channel, after respiration has ceased and before the ceasing of the inner breath. Ordinary people describe this state as "loss of consciousness."

The duration of this experience of inner radiance is uncertain, for it depends on the health and characteristics of the dying person's physical constitution, and on the degree of his or her proficiency in the practices related to the vital energies and channels. For those who have considerable practical experience, or those who have achieved stability in the practice of calm abiding, or those who have healthy energy channels, this experience can be prolonged.[11] In striving to make this introduction, therefore, one should remind the deceased repeatedly by giving the instruction as above and below, until serous fluid emerges from the apertures of the sense organs. For those persons of great negativity and those classes of beings with unhealthy channels, this phase lasts no longer than a single snapping of the fingers. In others, it may last for as long as it takes to eat a meal. However, as most sūtras and tantras state that the period of unconsciousness following the moment of death may last for three and a half days, generally one should persevere for that length of time, in making this introduction to inner radiance.

As for the way in which this introduction is made: if capable, the dying person should facilitate this of his or her own accord by projecting a formerly cultivated spiritual practice into the intermediate state. If the individual is not capable of this, then a spiritual teacher, a student, or a spiritual sibling who was a close friend should stay nearby and clearly remind the dying person of the signs of death in their correct sequence, saying:

.   .   .

Now, the sign of the dissolution of earth into water is present, of water into fire, fire into wind, wind into consciousness . . .

.   .   .

and so forth as set down in the text entitled "Natural Liberation Through Recognition of the Visual Indications and Signs of Death."

Then, when the sequence of the signs is almost complete, the attendant should encourage the dying person to cultivate the following altruistic intention, beginning with the words: "O Child of Buddha Nature!" or, if the dying person is a spiritual teacher, the attendant should gently say the following words into the ear:

.   .   .

O Venerable One! I beg you not to be distracted from the cultivation of an altruistic intention!

.   .   .

If the dying person is a spiritual sibling or anyone else, the attendant should call to him or her by name and say the following words:

.   .   .

O Child of Buddha Nature, that which is called death has now arrived. Therefore you should adopt an altruistic motivation and concentrate your thinking as follows: "I have arrived at the time of death, so now, relying on the process of death, I will single-mindedly cultivate an altruistic intention. I will meditate on the generation of loving kindness, compassion, and an altruistic intention to attain enlightenment. For the benefit of all sentient beings, who are as limitless as space, I must attain perfect buddhahood." And in particular, you should think: "At this moment, for the sake of all sentient beings, I must recognize the time of death as the arising of inner radiance, the Buddha-body of Reality, and while in that state I must attain the supreme accomplishment of the Great Seal, and thereby act for the good of all sentient beings. If I do not achieve this accomplishment, then, recognizing the intermediate state as it is, I will actualize the coalescent Buddha-body of the Great Seal during the intermediate state, and thereby, manifesting in order to instruct each in accordance with his or her needs, I will act for the benefit of all sentient beings, who are as limitless as space." Without giving up the focus on cultivating an altruistic intention, in the above way, recollect the meditative experiences that you formerly developed on the basis of the oral teachings.

·   ·   ·

Those words should be clearly spoken, while placing the lips close to the ear of the dying person. Without permitting the attention of the dying one to be distracted even for an instant, the attendant should remind him or her of past meditative experiences.

Then, when the respiration has ceased, and the two carotid arteries have been firmly pressed, remind the dying person with the following words, if the individual was a spiritual teacher or a spiritual friend greater than oneself:

·   ·   ·

Venerable One! The inner radiance of the ground is now arisen before you. Recognize it, and concentrate directly on its experiential cultivation.

·   ·   ·

For all others, one should introduce the inner radiance of the ground with the following words:

·   ·   ·

O Child of Buddha Nature, (*call the name of the individual*), listen! Pure inner radiance, reality itself, is now arising before you.

Recognize it! O Child of Buddha Nature, this radiant essence that is now your conscious awareness is a brilliant emptiness. It is beyond substance, beyond characteristics, and beyond color, completely empty of inherent existence in any respect whatsoever. This is the female buddha Samantabhadrī, the essential nature of reality. The essence of your own conscious awareness is emptiness. Yet this is not a vacuous or nihilistic emptiness; this, your very own conscious awareness, is unimpededly radiant, brilliant, and vibrant. This conscious awareness is the male buddha Samantabhadra. The utterly indivisible presence of these two— the essence of your own awareness, which is empty, without inherent existence with respect to any substance whatsoever; and your own conscious awareness, which is vibrant and radiantly present—is the Buddha-body of Reality. This intrinsic awareness, manifest in a great mass of light, in which radiance and emptiness are indivisible, is the buddha nature of unchanging light, beyond birth or death. Just to recognize this is enough! If you recognize this brilliant essence of your own conscious awareness to be the buddha nature, then to gaze into intrinsic awareness is to abide in the enlightened intention of all the buddhas.

· · ·

This introduction should be made three or seven times, with correct pronunciation and clear diction. Accordingly, the deceased will first recollect the teachings as they had been formerly given by his or her teacher, and second be introduced to inner radiance as a naked natural awareness. And then, third, having recognized this, he or she will attain the Buddha-body of Reality, beyond conjunction or disjunction, and certainly achieve liberation. Recognition of the first inner radiance of the ground takes place in this way.

LOSS

TRANSFORMING BEREAVEMENT IN
THE MIRROR OF GUIDANCE

Even though it is now more than thirty years since I first read the following chapter of *The Tibetan Book of the Dead*, I still find this masterful text a potent, continuing source of inspiration.

Presented here is a compelling metaphorical narrative illustrating the processes of our cognitive state in death, interlaced with advice on how we may interpret and creatively address these experiences. Also presented is a way of conceiving of death, guidance on how to approach our own death with composure, and a transforming perspective on bereavement.

As we read this chapter, we also discover that the text reveals a penetrating insight into the nature of each moment of our present waking state.

Here, at the core of the description of the after-death state, we see again the now familiar pattern of the mind's natural dynamic—of moving from a nonconceptual state, to a subtle dreamlike state, to a physical waking state—dramatically described as the journey from the moment of death, through a dreamlike intermediate state, to rebirth.

If we watch our minds very closely in the present moment, we can see how, out of the nonconceptual pure awareness that underlies all our thoughts, the sense of our own physical presence or "I-ness" arises first. Instantly, our minds become conditioned by our own mental habits and memories, and then suddenly our entire sensory and mental landscape is established, filled with our moment-by-moment expectations and emotions.

Interestingly, we also see this same process—an entire mindscape arising from a pure, luminous awareness—in both the following description of the after-death state, and in recent medical accounts of how the near-death experience unfolds.

As described in the previous chapter, those who have reported a near-death experience commonly recount being enveloped by a clear, radiant luminosity, which, following the consciousness leaving the body, fills their field of vision. This stage is often described as being accompanied by a sense of timeless spaciousness, a feeling of completeness, and of being enveloped by a loving presence. In this "out of body" state an awareness arises of being "just a mind" with a body that is insubstantial and weightless. Both in our text and in near-death reports, this dreamlike body is described as having the ability to see and hear clearly, as being able to travel wherever it wishes, and to pass effortlessly through physical objects. Again, our text and the near-death reports both describe how our existence in this subtle body develops. Following a period of remaining aware of the place and the physical body we have left behind, gradually memories of one's past life begin to dominate our experience and, as this flood of vivid recollections builds, it culminates in a "life review" in which the consequences of our actions in life are revealed.

Sogyal Rinpoche, in his *Tibetan Book of Living and Dying*, discusses in some detail the parallels between the near-death experience and the description of the after-death state in *The Tibetan Book of the Dead*. The similarities are striking. Three of the main characteristics of the after-death state and the near-death state have clear parallels: the meeting with a powerful luminosity, the arising in a dreamlike body, and the consequent surge of memories culminating in a life review, which brings insight into the consequences of our actions during our lives. Similarly, just as our normal daily pattern of awareness moves from deep sleep, passes through a dream state, and then emerges into a physical waking state, we see in the near-death reports an underlying cyclical pattern of the individual's awareness moving from a radiant luminosity, to an "out of body" dreamlike experience, and then reentering the physical body.

Perhaps, though, one of the most challenging aspects of the description of the after-death state in *The Tibetan Book of the Dead* is the idea that death holds up an all-seeing mirror, "the mirror of past actions," to our eyes. In this deep-seeing reflection, the consequences of all our negative and positive actions in life are clearly seen and there is a weighing of our past actions in the light of their consequences. This "life review" process, which parallels that described in near-death experiences, is metaphorically described in our text as the weighing of white pebbles, representing our positive actions, against the weight of black pebbles, representing our negative actions. The poet Heathcote Williams has come up with a wonderful phrase that elegantly illustrates this process: "death develops life's photographs." This is a hard concept to embrace—because in our daily life we usually remain somewhat oblivious to the consequences of our actions. But even here, there is a parallel with our normal day-to-day experience, because if we look at our minds closely, we can see that as a new cluster of thoughts and emotions comes into our mind, we do experience a sense of "conscience" that modulates our array of often conflicting thoughts and emotions. Before we speak or act, we usually weigh divergent thoughts and emotions before we decide on what we will say or do next. This process, in which we judge our own thoughts and emotions and on the basis of which we then allow ourselves to be propelled into our next mental state or act, is a kind of "inner or self-judgment" and it is a normal process of the mind.

In death, of course, this process of "life review" and "inner judgment" is vast—because it is said to encompass our own innermost insight into the entirety of our life's experience. In our text, this process of the mind developing an expanded awareness of all our actions and their consequences is metaphorically described as our being devoured by Yama, the Buddhist "Lord of Death," the embodiment of the forces of impermanence and the inexorable laws of cause and effect. Being devoured then leads to the experience of one's dreamlike body being repeatedly cut into pieces, spontaneously revived, and then cut into pieces again and again. Carl Jung, in his psychological commentary on the 1927 partial translation of *The Tibetan Book of the Dead*, succinctly describes this process as the "disintegration of the envelope of the self" and the "abolishing of the normal checks imposed by the conscious mind and the giving of unlimited scope to the play of the unconscious."

Thankfully though, as in life, this process of the mind being flooded by usually suppressed or unconscious conflicting thoughts, emotions, and memories, is followed by a natural coalescence, the arrival at a new inner balance. As our text emphasizes, this is a crucial determining stage. Just as we are about to enter a changed emotive state, it is essential that we recognize the nature of our own fundamental reality: everything we experience comes through, and is dependent on, our own mind. Our experience from moment to moment is the result of our own mental and emotional habits; it is not coming from anywhere else. At this crucial stage, the guidance in our text comes back to the same theme again and again. Our experience is the product of our own mental constructs, it is we who choose how we interpret our own experience, and we do therefore have an extraordinary freedom and opportunity. We are not trapped by our own experience—we are our own jailer, with the key in our hand. Whether from moment to moment we enter into an emotive state, engulfed by elation, jealousy, pride, confusion, blankness, desire, craving, anger, hatred, or fear, is ultimately our own choice. In our text, these various states are depicted as the differing realms of existence into which we may pass at birth, but, as we know from our own experience, these are also the states we may feel compelled to enter from moment to moment in life.

Before my father passed away I felt confident that I could remain strong and be a source of comfort and support for my mother. I truly hoped also that I could be peaceful, centered, and strong for my father and not become lost in my own sense of loss. Initially, while caught up in all the activity of preparing for the funeral—speaking to our relatives, writing the eulogy, and designing my father's small grave—I felt calm and purposeful. In the first evenings and mornings after his death I sat on my bed and tried to hold my father in a sense of restful, open spaciousness. I tried to let my own mind settle into a peaceful, warm expanse and to allow this to envelop my sense of nearness to my father. Yet to my surprise, my feelings of loss soon manifested far more physically than I had expected. The physical sensation began with a feeling of numbness on the left side of the back of my head. Then, as if leaking from this strangely feelingless, cold, and empty space, an all-pervading sense of meaninglessness, a very deep sadness, began to flood through my body and mind. I truly wished that I could ease these deep feelings of separation and focus my mind on being a support for my father. Intellectually, I knew that my own feelings were being driven by my own attachments, stirred and made powerful by constantly being thrown into so many poignant memories of being with my father since childhood. I knew that my own fears of being alone, of being unable to find fulfillment in life, were made more piercing by the menacing unfamiliarity of losing a loved one. I also knew that I had to move through my own self-concern and to concentrate my motivation on helping my father and mother. Each day I would read the previous chapter and the chapter that follows and, holding my father in my thoughts, try to interpret for him the passages I felt would give him the greatest support. In my own fragile state, having been freshly born into this altered realm of bereavement, every aspect of the text took on an immediacy of meaning. As I rode on waves of poignant memories and felt cast to and fro, in just seconds, between sweetness and despair, the text spoke directly to me like an empathetic friend. Finding the soft ground of the space between my whirling thoughts, a sense of ease and purpose began to return.

We all know the amazingly simple joy that we experience when we can help another person—even if it is just in a small way and even if we are helping a stranger. The instinct to help others is one of the deepest of human propensities and the sense of fulfillment that we feel on helping another is one of the most uplifting and enduring. Finding this "sweet spot" of compassion at the time of loss can be deeply powerful. When a loved one dies, simply turning our emphasis toward supporting the loved one who has passed away can, in itself, be the greatest solace of all.

The chapter that follows comes from the final section of "The Great Liberation by Hearing." In many Tibetan Buddhist households it is read, together with the previous chapter, for a period of up to forty-nine days from the time of death and the moment of bereavement.

CHARACTERISTICS OF THE AFTER-DEATH STATE

O Child of Buddha Nature, when your mind and body separate, the pure luminous apparitions of reality itself will arise: subtle and clear, radiant and dazzling, naturally bright and awesome, shimmering like a mirage on a plain in summer. Do not fear them! Do not be terrified! Do not be awed! They are the natural luminosities of your own actual reality. Therefore recognize them as they are!

From within these lights, the natural sound of reality will resound, clear and thunderous, reverberating like a thousand simultaneous peals of thunder. This is the natural sound of your own actual reality. So, do not be afraid! Do not be terrified! Do not be awed! The body that you now have is called "a mental body," it is the product of subtle propensities and not a solid corporeal body of flesh and blood. This "body" is described in the *tantras:*

> *Having the bodily form of one's past and emergent existences,*

Complete with all sense faculties, and the power of unob-
structed movement.
    Endowed with miraculous abilities derived from past
actions,
    Visible to those similar in kind and through pure clairvoy-
ance.

Here, "past and emergent" means that your present body, which is a product of your past habitual tendencies, will resemble a body of flesh and blood, but, like a body of the auspicious aeon, it will also be radiant and possess certain of the major and minor marks. Since this state is an apparitional experience of the mental body, it is called "the mental body of apparitional experience in the intermediate state." At this time, if you are to be born as a god, you will come to experience the apparitional field of the realm of the gods. Depending on whichever of the realms you are to take birth in, whether that of the antigods, humans, animals, anguished spirits, or hell beings, you will come to experience its particular apparitional field. Therefore, "past" means that for three and a half days you will possess the bodily form that is a product of your past habitual tendencies and existences. And "emergent" means that, after three and a half days, the apparitional field of the next realm into which you are to be born will emerge. Hence the expression, "past and emergent" existences.

Whatever apparitional fields emerge at this time, do not be drawn by them! Do not become attached to them! Do not cling to them! If you cling to them and become attached, you will continue to roam among the six classes of beings and be turning toward suffering. Although, until yesterday, the intermediate state of reality arose within you, you did not recognize it. As a result you have been compelled to wander here. Now, just as was formerly introduced by your spiritual teacher, if you are able to cultivate, undistractedly, a recognition of the essential nature of reality, if you can rest and abide without grasping and without activity, directly, in the unwavering, naked awareness that is radiance and emptiness conjoined, you can attain liberation and avoid wandering yet further toward the womb entrances. If you are not able to achieve this recognition, then visualize your meditational deity, whichever it may be, or your spiritual teacher, as being seated on the crown of your head and be intensely and fervently devoted. This is most important. Again and again, do not be distracted.

. . .

If the deceased does indeed recognize this essential nature of reality, he or she will attain liberation and avoid roaming further among the six classes of beings. But, on account of negative past actions, recognition is not easy to achieve, and therefore one should reiterate the introduction in the following words:

. . .

O Child of Buddha Nature, listen carefully yet again! The phrase, "Complete with all sense faculties, and the power of unobstructed movement" means that, even though you may have been blind, deaf, or lame while you were alive, now, in the intermediate state, your eyes see forms, your ears hear sounds, and all your sense faculties are faultless, clear, and complete. Hence the *tantra* says, "Complete with all sense faculties." Recognize this sensory clarity, for it is a sign that you have died and are wandering in the intermediate state. Remember this oral instruction! O Child of Buddha Nature, "unobstructed" means that the body which you now have is a mental body. Your awareness is now separated from its physical support. Therefore, this is not a body of solid form. Accordingly, you now have the ability to move unobstructedly; penetrating to the core of all forms, you can pass through Mount Sumeru and through dwellings, the earth, stones, boulders, and mountains. Indeed, other than your mother's womb and the "indestructible seat,"[12] you can pass back and forth even through Mount Sumeru itself. Remember the advice of your spiritual teacher—for this ability is a sign that you are wandering in the intermediate state of rebirth. Recognize this and pray to the meditational deity Mahākāruṇika.

O Child of Buddha Nature, the phrase "endowed with miraculous abilities derived from past actions" does not mean that you necessarily possess any enlightened attributes, or any miraculous ability in meditative stability, but that you have a miraculous ability that results from your past actions and accords with your past actions. Consequently, you will have the ability to circumambulate Mount Sumeru and the four continents in an instant. Merely in the time it takes to withdraw or hold out an arm, you can travel instantly anywhere you wish, just by thinking of your desired destination. Do not be fascinated by these diverse and haphazard miraculous abilities. Do not indulge in them. Of all the things you have the ability to recall, there is not one that you cannot make manifest. You have the ability now to manifest any aspect of your past, unimpededly. Therefore recognize this and pray to your spiritual teacher.

O Child of Buddha Nature, as for the phrase "visible to those similar in kind and through pure clairvoyance," the words "similar in kind" mean that in the intermediate state those of a similar kind of birth will come to perceive one another. Thus, in the case of those "similar in kind" who are to be born as gods, the gods to be perceive one another. Similarly, those that are "similar in kind" to any of the six classes of beings will come to perceive one another. Do not become attached at the sight of these beings! Meditate on the meditational deity Mahākāruṇika. The words "visible through pure clairvoyance" do not refer to the clairvoyance that results from the meritorious qualities of the gods and so forth, but they do refer to the pure clairvoyance with which those of genuine meditative concentration perceive. However, this is not a clairvoyance that can perceive the beings of the intermediate state at all times. If you are intent on seeing beings of like nature in this intermediate state, then they will be perceived. If you are not so intent, they will not be perceived. This clairvoyance will dissolve as soon as your concentration is distracted.

O Child of Buddha Nature, with a body having qualities such as these just described, you will once again see your homeland and your relatives, as if in a dream. Yet even though you call out to your relatives, they will not reply. You will see your family and relatives crying and realize: "I am dead. What should I do now?" Thinking this, you will be overwhelmed by intense suffering—you will feel like a fish expelled from the water, writhing on hot sand. Although you will suffer on realizing that you are dead, this is not helpful to you now. If you have a spiritual teacher, pray to your spiritual teacher! Pray to the meditational deity Mahākāruṇika! Although you will feel attached to your relatives, this is not helpful to you now. Do not be attached! Pray to Mahākāruṇika, and be free of suffering, awe, and fear.

O Child of Buddha Nature, your present awareness, freed from its physical support, is being blown by the coursing vital energy of past actions. Choicelessly, riding the horse of breath, it drifts directionless, like a feather on the wind. To all those who are crying, you will call out: "I am here! Do not cry!" But they will not hear you. Yet again, you will realize "I am dead" and experience a very profound despair. Do not be absorbed by this suffering!

Continuously, there will be grayness, like autumn twilight, with neither day nor night. The intermediate states between death and birth will last for one week, or two, or three, or four, or five, or six, or seven weeks—up to forty-nine days in all. It is said that suffering in the intermediate state of rebirth will last, generally speaking, for twenty-one days. However, since the duration of this state is based on past actions, a specific number of days is not certain.

O Child of Buddha Nature, at this time the fierce, turbulent, utterly unbearable hurricane of past actions will be swirling behind you, driving you on. Do not be afraid! This is your own bewildered perception. Before you, there will be a terrifying, dense, and unfathomable darkness, echoing with cries of "Strike!" and "Kill!" Do not be afraid! Moreover, in the case of very negative beings, a swarm of carnivorous ogres will arise, executors of the unfailing law of cause and effect, brandishing an array of weapons, and screaming out aggressively "Strike!" and "Kill!" You will imagine that you are being pursued by terrifying wild animals. You will imagine that you are being pursued by hordes of people, and that you are struggling through snow, through rain, through blizzards, and through darkness. There will be the sound of mountains crumbling, of lakes flooding, of fire spreading, and the roar of fierce winds springing up. Terrified, you will try to flee wherever you can, but your path ahead will suddenly be cut off by three precipices: one white, one red, and one black, all three awesomely frightening; you will feel as if on the verge of falling.

O Child of Buddha Nature, these are not truly precipices. They are aversion, attachment, and delusion, respectively. Know now that this is the intermediate state of rebirth, and call to the meditational deity Mahākāruṇika by name, and pray: "O Lord Mahākāruṇika, Spiritual Teacher and Precious Jewel, save me (*say your name*) from falling into lower existences." Pray with deep commitment in this way; do not forget!

At this stage, in the case of those individuals who have gathered the accumulations of merit and pristine cognition and have sincerely practiced the teachings, one will be welcomed by visions of abundant riches and one will experience manifold blissful and happy states. In the case of those individuals who are indifferent or deluded, who have been neither virtuous nor negative, one will experience neither pleasure nor pain, but only an apathetic delusion. Whichever of these happens, O Child of Buddha Nature, whatever objects of desire or blissful or happy states appear before you, do not be attached to them. Do not cling to them! Be free from attachment and clinging and mentally offer these experiences to your spiritual teacher and to the Three Precious Jewels. Particularly, if these visions are of indifference, devoid of happiness or pain, abide in the experience of the Great Seal, where awareness is naturally present, without meditation and without distraction. This is very important.

O Child of Buddha Nature, at this time you will try to find shelter from the hurricane of past actions below bridges, in mansions, in temples or grass huts, or beside stūpas and so forth, but this shelter will be momentary, it will not last. Your awareness, now separated from your body, will not rest and you will feel reckless, angry, and afraid. Your consciousness will be faltering, superficial, and nebulous. Again you will realize: "Alas! I am dead, what should I do now?" Reflecting on this, your consciousness will grow sad, your heart will be chilled, and you will feel intense and boundless misery. Your mind is being compelled to move on, without settling in one place. Do not indulge in all kinds of memories! Let your awareness rest in an undistracted state!

The time will come when you will realize that you have no food, except that which has been dedicated to you. As for companionship, here, similarly, there will be no certainty. These are both indications that the mental body is wandering in the intermediate state of rebirth. Your present feelings of happiness and sorrow are now driven by your past actions.

Once again, seeing your homeland, circle of friends, relatives, and even your own corpse, you will realize: "I am dead! What should I do now?" You will feel deeply saddened by your existence in a mental body and wish, "O that I might obtain a physical body!" Consequently, you will experience roaming here and there in search of a body. You might even attempt, many times, to reenter your own body, but a long time has already elapsed in the previous intermediate state of reality. In winter your body will have frozen, in summer it will have decayed. Alternatively, your relatives will have cremated it, buried it in a grave, or offered it to the birds and wild animals. Not finding a way back, you will feel utterly distressed, and you will certainly feel yourself trying to squeeze into the crevices between stones and rocks. Torments such as these will enfold you. This being the intermediate state of rebirth, so long as you search for a body you will experience nothing but suffering. Therefore give up your clinging to a body and rest in a state of nonactivity, undistractedly.

BALANCING LIGHT AND DARK

Liberation can be obtained in the intermediate state as a result of the above introduction. However, even though this introduction is given, due to negative past actions, recognition may not occur. So again, you should call to the deceased by name and say the following words:

.   .   .

O Child of Buddha Nature, (*call to the deceased by name*), listen to me. It is due to your own past actions that you are now suffering in this way. No one else is responsible—this is solely the result of your own past actions. Pray ardently now to the Three Precious

Jewels. They will protect you. If you do not pray intensely now, especially if you do not know how to meditate on the Great Seal, or if you cannot meditate on a meditational deity, the "innate good conscience" within you will now gather together all your virtuous actions, counting them out with white pebbles, and the "innate bad conscience" within you will gather together all your nonvirtuous actions, counting them out with black pebbles. At this moment you will tremble with extreme fear, awe, and terror. You will tell lies, saying, "I have not committed nonvirtuous actions!" But at this, Yama will say: "I shall consult the mirror of past actions." In the mirror of past actions, all your virtues and nonvirtues will be reflected vividly and precisely. Your attempts at deceit will be of no use. Tying a rope around your neck, Yama will drag you forward. He will sever your head at the neck, extract your heart, pull out your entrails, lick your brains, drink your blood, eat your flesh, and suck your bones. Despite this, you will not die. Even as your body is repeatedly cut into pieces, it will be continuously revived. Experiencing being cut into pieces in this way, time after time, will cause enormous suffering. From the moment the counting of the pebbles begins, do not be afraid! Do not be terrified! Do not lie, and do not be afraid of Yama. The body you now have is a mental body; therefore, even though you experience being slain and cut into pieces, you cannot die. Recognize now that, in reality, you need have no fear, because, in truth, your body is a natural form of emptiness. The acolytes of Yama are also, in reality, natural forms of emptiness—these are your own bewildered perceptions. Your body, formed of mental propensities, is a natural form of emptiness. Emptiness cannot harm emptiness. Signlessness cannot harm signlessness. Outside, and distinct from your own bewildering perceptions, Yama, gods, malevolent forces, the bull-headed Rakṣa, and so on, do not substantially exist. Recognize this! Recognize, now, that this is the intermediate state! Place your mind in the meditative stability of the Great Seal! If you do not know how to meditate, directly examine the essence of that which is producing your fear and terror. This essence is a stark emptiness, completely without inherent existence in any respect whatsoever! This stark emptiness is the Buddha-body of Reality. Yet, this emptiness is not a vacuous or nihilistic emptiness. The essential nature of this emptiness is an awesome, direct, and radiant awareness, which is the enlightened intention of the Buddha-body of Perfect Resource. Indeed, emptiness and radiance are not separate: the essential nature of emptiness is radiance and the essential nature of radiance is emptiness. This indivisible, naked, unclouded, and exposed awareness, present as it is right now in a natural uncontrived state, is the Buddha-body of Essentiality. Furthermore, the natural expressive power of this Buddha-body of Essentiality is the compassionate Buddha-body of Emanation, which arises everywhere without obstruction.

O Child of Buddha Nature, listen to me now, and do not be distracted. By merely recognizing the essential nature of your experience in the above way, you will attain perfect buddhahood, endowed with these four buddha-bodies. Do not be distracted! The division between buddhas and sentient beings is determined by this recognition. If you are distracted at this critical moment, the opportunity to escape from the swamp of suffering will be lost. It is said of this very moment:

In an instant, penetrating analysis is made.
In an instant, perfect buddhahood is attained.

Until yesterday, because you were distracted, even though so many aspects of the intermediate states have arisen, you did not attain recognition. Up to this time, you have experienced so much fear and terror. Now, if you continue to be distracted, the lifeline of compassion, suspended to you, will be cut off and you will move on to a place where there is no immediate prospect of liberation. So be careful.

.   .   .

Through this introduction, even though the deceased may have failed to attain recognition previously, he or she will be able to do so at this stage and consequently attain liberation.

If, however, the deceased is a layperson, who does not know how to meditate, you should say the following words:

.   .   .

O Child of Buddha Nature, if you do know how to meditate you should call to mind the Buddha, the sacred teachings, the sublime assembly of monks and nuns, and the meditational deity Mahākāruṇika and pray to them. Meditate on all the fearful and terrifying appearances as being forms of Mahākāruṇika, or your meditational deity. Remember your spiritual teacher and remember the name that you received during empowerment ceremonies in the human world. Say this name to Yama Dharmarāja and do not be afraid of him. Know, now, that even if you were to plunge down over the precipices, you would not be harmed. So, abandon your fear and your terror.

. . .

Even though liberation may not have been achieved previously, if the above introduction is accepted, the deceased will attain liberation at this juncture.

Yet since there is the possibility that the deceased will not achieve recognition, even though the introduction has been given, it is very important to persevere. Therefore, once again, one should call to the deceased by name and say the following words:

. . .

O Child of Buddha Nature, your present perceptions can, like a catapult, in an instant cast you into the most awesome states, either blissful or full of suffering. Therefore, now, it is critical that your perceptions are not colored by either attachment or aversion.

It may be that you are about to take birth in the higher realms, yet at the time when the perceptions of the higher realms occur, your living relatives, now left behind, are sacrificing and offering many animals on your behalf, dedicating this activity to you, the deceased. Corrupted perceptions will thus arise and consequently an intense aversion may well up within you, and this will form a connecting link to a birth in the hell realms. Therefore, whatever activities occur in the place that you have left behind, meditate on loving kindness, and ensure that aversion does not arise!

Alternatively, your mind may grow attached to your wealth

and possessions, now left behind, or else, knowing that your wealth and possessions are being enjoyed and owned by others, you may become both attached to those worldly goods and also hateful toward those left behind who are using your possessions. As a result of this, a connecting link will certainly be formed to a birth among the hell beings or among the anguished spirits, even though you may have been at the point of attaining birth in one of the higher realms. However attached you may be to the wealth now left behind, you do not have the ability to enjoy it. Since it is absolutely of no use to you, abandon your attachment and yearning for the wealth that you have left behind. Let it go! Be decisive! Regardless of who is enjoying your wealth, do not be possessive! Let it go! Cultivate devotion, and imagine that you are offering these worldly possessions to your spiritual teacher and to the Three Precious Jewels. Rest in a state free from attachment and free from clinging.

Once again, even when the *Kaṅkaṇīdhāraṇī* incantation for the dead is being recited for you and the "Purification of the Lower Realms" is being recited on your behalf, you may perceive, with your present subtle cognitive ability, that these rites are being performed impurely and distractedly, and that those who are performing these rituals are impure in both their commitments and vows and are careless in their conduct. As a result, you may have no confidence in them, you may form a bad opinion of them, and you may become fearfully and horribly aware of their negative past actions, etc., as well as of their impure practice of the sacred teachings and the rituals. Feeling this, you will experience the utmost sadness, and think: "Alas, they have betrayed me! They have truly betrayed me!" As a consequence of your profound disenchantment, instead of maintaining purity of perception and feelings of respect, negative opinions and loss of confidence will arise within you. Thus, these perceptions and feelings will form a connecting link that will certainly propel you into the lower existences, and, in this way, your subtle cognitive ability and the rituals recited on your behalf will not have been of benefit, but rather of great harm.

However impure may be the practice of the sacred teachings by your friends now left behind, you must maintain respect and purity of perception from the depths of your heart. Think to yourself: "My own perception is so polluted! How could the speech of the buddhas be impure! These impure perspectives have arisen as a consequence of my own impure perception, and will appear to me just as the flaws on my face will be reflected in a mirror. As for these individuals performing the rituals, in reality their bodies are the sublime community of monks and nuns, their speech is the genuine sacred teaching, and their minds are the essence of the buddhas. Therefore, I take refuge in them." Thinking thus, whatever activities occur in the place that you have left behind, they will certainly be beneficial to you. It is extremely important to maintain this purity of perception. Do not forget this!

Even if you are about to be born into the lower existences, if you maintain purity of perception, and you perceive the relatives that you have left behind practicing the virtuous teachings, unstained by negativity, and you see your spiritual teachers and masters purely practicing the rituals with virtuous body, speech, and mind, you will feel great joy. Simply through this experience of great joy, even though you were about to fall into lower existences, this joy will form a connecting link, which will certainly turn you back toward the higher realms. Since there is such manifold benefit, do not now lapse into impure perception. It is extremely important to maintain purity of perception and to be unbiasedly devoted. So, be careful!

O Child of Buddha Nature, in short, since your awareness during this intermediate state lacks any material support, it is light and volatile, and therefore, whatever virtuous or nonvirtuous perceptions arise, these are very powerful. Do not be absorbed by nonvirtuous thoughts! Call to mind the virtuous practices of your past! Even if you did not engage in virtuous practices during your life, maintain purity of perception and deep devotion! Pray to your meditational deity or to Mahākāruṇika, and with a powerful longing repeat the following aspirational prayer:

> *Now when I roam alone, separated from loved ones,*
> *And myriad images of emptiness arise, naturally manifesting,*
> *May the buddhas quickly release the power of their compassion,*
> *And may the fear of the awesome and terrifying intermediate state be annulled.*
>
> *When I experience suffering, as the result of negative past actions,*
> *May the meditational deity Mahākāruṇika dispel all such misery,*

And as the natural sound of reality reverberates like a thousand peals of thunder,
May all sounds be transformed into the resonance of the Six Syllables.

When I am driven on by past actions, unable to find a refuge,
May the Great Compassionate One, Mahākāruṇika, protect me,
And as I experience the suffering of habitual tendencies and past actions,
May the meditative stabilities of inner radiance and bliss naturally arise.

Say this aspirational prayer with ardent longing; it will certainly lead you on to the path. Be absolutely certain that this aspirational prayer will not deceive you. This is most important!

.   .   .

Through these words, the deceased will regain his or her focus, and recognition will occur. Then, liberation will be attained.

MOVING TOWARD A NEW BIRTH

Even though this introduction may have been given many times, due to the potency of strong negative past actions, recognition may be difficult. It is very beneficial, therefore, to repeat the introduction now, many times. Again, therefore, calling to the deceased by name, you should say the following words at least three times:

.   .   .

O Child of Buddha Nature, if you have not taken to heart the introduction that has gone before, from now on the body of your past life will grow more faint and the body of your next life will grow more vivid. At this, you will be dismayed, and you will think: "I am experiencing such misery! Now I will look for whatever kind of body I can find." Thinking in this way, you will move haphazardly and randomly toward whatever might appear and consequently the six lights indicative of the six realms of living beings will dawn; and, according to your past actions, the light of the realm into which you are to be born will shine the most of all. O Child of Buddha Nature, listen! What are these six lights, you may ask? A dull white light indicative of the realm of the gods will arise. A dull red light indicative of the realm of the antigods will arise. A dull blue light indicative of the human realm will arise. A dull green light indicative of the animal realm will arise. A dull yellow light indicative of the realm of the anguished spirits will arise, and a dull smoky light indicative of the realm of the hell beings will arise. These six lights will emerge. And at this time, your present body will take on the color of the light of the realm into which you are to be born. O Child of Buddha Nature, at this juncture, the essential points of the oral instructions are extremely important.

Meditate now on the light that dawns as being Mahākāruṇika!

Meditate on the thought that when the light dawns, it is Mahākāruṇika. This is the most profound crucial point. It is extremely important, because this oral instruction obstructs birth.

Alternatively, you should meditate for a long time on your meditational deity, whichever it may be. Meditate on the deity appearing like an illusion, completely free from inherent existence. This is called the practice of the "pure illusion-like body." Accordingly, dissolve the form of the meditational deity from the extremities inward until it disappears completely, and abide in the resultant state of emptiness and radiance, where nothing at all substantially exists and where there is no subjective apprehension. Meditate yet again on the meditational deity. Meditate again on the inner radiance. Meditate alternately in this way, and, after this, dissolve your awareness itself from the extremities inward, into emptiness and radiance. Wherever there is space there is awareness. Wherever there is awareness there is the Buddha-body of Reality. Abide nakedly, therefore, in the state of the unimpeded Buddha-body of Reality, free from conceptual elaboration. Abiding in this state, birth will be obstructed and buddhahood will be attained.

.   .   .

Yet those unfamiliar with meditative experience and those very weak in their practice will not be able to understand and apply the above introductions. Once again, overcome by confusion, they will wander toward the womb entrances. Thus, the teachings that obstruct the womb entrances become of great importance and you should, once again, call to the deceased by name and say the following words:

·   ·   ·

O Child of Buddha Nature, if you have not attained recognition as a result of the introductions that have gone before, then, based on the potency of your past actions, the perception will arise that you are moving upward, or moving horizontally, or moving downward. As this occurs, you should meditate on Mahākāruṇika. Remember this!

Yet again, as described before, the experience will arise of being pursued by whirlwinds, blizzards, hail, or fog, and a crowd of people, and you will be trying to escape. Those who are lacking in merit will experience that they are fleeing toward a place of suffering. Those with merit will experience arriving at a place of happiness. O Child of Buddha Nature, now, at this point, the signs of the environment into which you are to be born, on one among the four continents, will arise. Specifically for this moment, there are many profound essential points of oral instruction. Therefore listen, now, without distraction. Even though, previously, you have not taken to heart the essential instructions introduced to you, you can do so now, for even those whose practice is very weak can understand and apply one of the following essential instructions. So listen, now, without distraction.

At this stage, it is extremely important that you carefully employ the methods for obstructing the womb entrances. Principally, there are two such methods of obstruction. These are: first, the method that obstructs the person who is to enter the womb and, second, the methods that obstruct the womb that is to be entered.

.   .   .

The oral teaching for the method that obstructs the person who is to enter the womb is as follows:

.   .   .

O Child of Buddha Nature, (*call to the deceased by name*), visualize now your meditational deity, whichever it may be, with vibrancy. Meditate on the deity as vividly apparent, yet completely lacking in inherent existence, like the reflection of the moon in water. If you do not have a specific meditational deity, then visualize the Lord Mahākāruṇika, again with great vibrancy. Then, gradually, dissolve the image of the meditational deity from the extremities inward, until it disappears completely and then meditate on the resultant union of inner radiance and emptiness, which is utterly free from any objective referent. This is the profound essential point. Meditate in this way, for it is said that by this means entry into a womb will be averted.

.   .   .

Should even this introduction not cause obstruction and should the deceased continue to draw closer to the act of entering a womb, there are also the profound oral instructions that obstruct the womb entrances. These are as follows:

.   .   .

O Child of Buddha Nature, listen carefully! In the recitation of the "Root Verses of the Six Intermediate States," the following lines are spoken. Repeat these, now, after me:

> *Alas, now as the intermediate state of rebirth arises before me,*
> *I must with one-pointed intention concentrate my mind,*
> *And resolutely connect with the residual potency of my virtuous past actions.*
> *I must obstruct the womb entrances and call to mind the methods of reversal.*
> *This is the time when perseverance and purity of perception are imperative.*
> *I must give up all jealousy and meditate on my spiritual teacher with consort.*

It is extremely important to clearly repeat these verses aloud, to arouse your memories of past virtues, to meditate on this prayer, and to experientially cultivate its meaning. The meaning of these verses is as follows: the line "now as the intermediate state of rebirth arises before me" explains that you are now roaming in the intermediate state of rebirth. As an indication of this, if you look into water, you will not see your reflection. Your body does not even cast a shadow. These are both signs that you do not have a solid body of flesh and blood, but that you are roaming, with a subtle mental body, in the intermediate state of rebirth.

Now, therefore, you "must with one-pointed intention concentrate your mind," undistractedly. At this moment, this singularity of intention is by itself the most important factor. It is like a horse being controlled by the use of a bridle. Whatever your intention focuses upon, this will come about. Do not turn your mind to negative past actions! Call to mind, now, your connections in the human world with the sacred teachings and instructions, remember the empowerments and oral transmissions previously received, remember your connection with this "Great Liberation by Hearing in the Intermediate States," and so forth. It is extremely important that you "resolutely connect with the residual potency of your virtuous past actions." Do not forget! Do not be distracted! The present moment is the dividing line between progression and regression. The present moment is the time when, by lapsing into laziness, even for an instant, you will experience constant suffering. The present moment is the time when, by concentrating with a singular intention, you will achieve constant happiness. Concentrate your mind with a single-pointed intention. "Resolutely connect with the residual potency of your virtuous past actions."

Now is the time when you must obstruct the womb entrances. It is said in the verses that you "must obstruct the womb entrances and call to mind the methods of reversal. This is the time when perseverance and purity of perception are imperative." You have now arrived at that stage. Your priority now is to obstruct the womb entrances. There are five methods that will bring about obstruction of the womb entrances, so keep them carefully in mind.

O Child of Buddha Nature, at this stage, the perception will arise of a male and a female engaging in sexual intercourse. Upon perceiving this, do not enter between the male and the female, but be mindful and "meditate on" the male and the female as being your "spiritual teacher with consort." Prostrate yourself before them and make offerings, projecting these from your mind. Be intensely devoted and request instructions from your spiritual teacher and consort. Just by intently focusing your thought in this way, the womb entrances will certainly be obstructed.

Should the womb entrances not be successfully obstructed through this method and you are nonetheless drawn ever nearer to entering the womb, then meditate now on the spiritual teacher and consort as being your personal meditational deities, whichever these may be, or, if you do not have a personal meditational deity, meditate on the spiritual teacher and consort as being Mahākāruṇika and his consort. Again, make offerings, projecting these from your mind and generate the thought very intently: "I request the attainment of your spiritual accomplishment!" Thereby, the womb entrances will be obstructed.

Should even this not obstruct the womb entrances, and you are still drawn ever nearer to entering the womb, the third method, which reverses attachment and aversion, is now to be revealed to you. There are four modes of birth: birth from an egg, birth from a womb, supernormal birth, and birth from warmth and moisture. Among these, the birth from an egg and birth from a womb are very similar, in that in both cases you will see the male and the female engaged in sexual union, as described above. If, based on either attachment or aversion, you enter a womb at this time, you will be born as a horse, bird, dog, human, or whatever is appropriate. If you are to be born as a male, you will experience the perceptions of a male. You will feel intense aversion toward the father and you will feel jealousy and attachment toward the mother. If you are to be born as a female, you will experience the perceptions of a female. You will feel intense envy and jealousy toward the mother and you will feel intense attachment and affection toward the father. This emotional arousal will cause you to enter a womb. Here you will experience the "coemergent delight," in the midst of the meeting between the sperm and the ovum. From that state of bliss you will faint into unconsciousness, and as time passes the embryo will come to maturity in the womb, moving through its various stages of development, that is, the clotting of the embryo, the oval elongation of the embryo, and so forth until, finally, you will emerge from the womb and open your eyes. Now, you will have turned into a puppy. Previously having been a human being, you will now have become a dog. So, consequently, you will suffer in a dog kennel, or, similarly, in a pigsty, or an anthill, or a wormhole, or else you may be born as a baby bull, a goat, a sheep, and so forth. There is no way back. You will experience all manner of sufferings in a state of great obscurity and delusion. Through this process you will continue to remain within the six classes of living beings, including the realms of the hell beings and the anguished spirits. You will be completely drained by boundless sufferings. There is nothing more awesome or frightening than this! Oh dear! This is truly terrifying! Oh dear, Oh dear, in this way, those who lack the oral instruction of a genuine spiritual teacher will indeed fall into the great abyss of cyclic existence and be tortured unbearably by continuous sufferings. Rather than this, listen to my words! Understand this instruction of mine. I will reveal now an oral instruction that obstructs the womb entrances, through the reversal of attachment and the reversal of aversion. Listen and understand this well! It is said in the "Root Verses of the Six Intermediate States:"

> I must obstruct the womb entrances and call to mind the methods of reversal.
> This is the time when perseverance and purity of perception are imperative.
> I must give up all jealousy and meditate on my spiritual teacher with consort.

As is described in the oral instruction above, if you are to be born as a male, you will feel attachment toward the mother and aversion toward the father. If you are to be born as a female, you will feel attachment to the father and aversion toward the mother. Thus you will come to experience jealousy, a conflict of attachment and aversion. Specific to this stage, there is a profound oral instruction. O Child of Buddha Nature, when the feelings of attachment and aversion arise, meditate as follows: "Alas, sentient beings such as I, with such negative past actions, have, up until now, roamed in cyclic existence. I have continued to wander in this way, being driven on by my feelings of attachment and aversion. If, especially at this time, I continue to be influenced by attachment and aversion, there is a danger that I will roam into the limitlessly diverse states of cyclic existence and risk sinking into the ocean of suffering, for a very long time. Therefore, now, from the very beginning, I must not generate attachment or aversion. Oh dear, Oh dear! As of now, I shall never again be motivated by attachment or aversion." By concentrating intently on this thought, as it is said in the tantras, the womb entrances will be obstructed by this singular intent alone. O Child of Buddha Nature, do not be distracted! Concentrate your mind on this thought, with a one-pointed intention.

. . .

Yet if, even having done this, the womb entrances are still not obstructed and the deceased draws ever nearer to entering a womb, then the womb entrances should be obstructed by giving the oral instruction on the unreal and illusion-like nature of all phenomena:

. . .

O Child of Buddha Nature, meditate in the following way! "Alas! The father and the mother in sexual union, the rain, the blackness, the hurricane, the thunderous sound, the fearful and terrifying experiences—the nature of these and of all phenomena is illusion-like. In whatever form phenomena arise, they are not real. All substantial things are unreal and false, like a mirage. They are not permanent. They are not changeless. So what is the purpose of my attachment to these perceptions? What is the purpose of my awe and terror? That which is nonexistent, I am seeing as existent! In reality, all these things that I perceive are the perceptions of my own mind. Yet the essential nature of mind is primordially nonexistent, like an illusion. So how is it possible for things to exist externally, in their own right? Since I have not understood this before, I have always regarded the nonexistent as

existent. I have regarded the unreal as real. I have regarded illusions as truth. This is why I have roamed in cyclic existence for such
a long time. Now, yet again, if I do not realize that all these phenomena are illusions, I will continue to roam in cyclic existence,
interminably, and without doubt I will drown in a swamp of every
manner of suffering. Now, I must realize that all these phenomena are completely devoid of substantial existence, even for a single
instant. In reality, they are like a dream, like an illusion, like an
echo, like a celestial city, like a mirage, like a reflection, like an
optical illusion, like the moon reflected in water. It is absolutely
certain that these phenomena are not truly real, but that they are
false. Through this singular resolve, I will blow apart my apprehension of their true existence. Through utter confidence in this
meditation, my apprehension of self-existence will be reversed."
By knowing from the depths of your heart that all these phenomena are unreal, the womb entrances will certainly be obstructed.

.   .   .

However, if, despite this teaching being given, the apprehension
of true existence is not shattered, and the womb entrances are
therefore not obstructed and the deceased draws ever nearer to
entering a womb, then there is a final profound oral instruction:

.   .   .

O Child of Buddha Nature, if, even after having engaged in the
above meditation, the womb entrances have still not been obstructed, now, according to the fifth profound oral instruction,
you must obstruct the womb entrances by meditating on inner

radiance. The method of meditation is as follows: "Alas! All seemingly substantial phenomena are expressions of my own mind. Yet in reality, this mind is of the nature of emptiness, it is beyond creation and beyond cessation." By focusing your thought in this way, your mind should naturally return to an uncontrived and stainless state. Let the mind rest in this, its natural state, directly in itself, in the same way, for example, as water is poured into water. Let the mind rest in its natural flow, clear, unconstricted, uncontrived, and relaxed. By following this method you can be sure that the womb entrances to the four modes of birth will certainly be obstructed. Meditate again and again in this way, until the womb entrances are closed.

.   .   .

Set down above are several profound and genuine instructions for effecting the obstruction of the womb entrances. For those with high, average, or low ability it is impossible not to be liberated by these instructions. This is because: first, consciousness in the intermediate state is endowed with an, albeit corrupt, supernormal cognitive ability. Therefore, whatever one says to the deceased is heard by the deceased. Second, even if the deceased was deaf or blind while in the human world, now, in the intermediate state, all the sensory faculties will be complete and therefore whatever is said will be apprehended. Third, since the deceased is continually being overwhelmed by fear and terror, there is an undistracted concentration on what to do; therefore, what is said will be listened to. Fourth, since the consciousness has no physical support, it is easy to guide and it can penetrate to the essence of whatever is focused upon. Additionally, since the power of retention is now many times clearer, even the mentally weak will have, in the intermediate state, a lucid awareness, by virtue of their past actions. Hence, they will have the gift of knowing how to meditate on that which is taught and the gift to assimilate such points of instruction. These are the reasons why the performance of rituals on behalf of the dead is beneficial. Indeed, it is extremely important to persevere in the reading aloud of this "Great Liberation by Hearing in the Intermediate States" for the entire forty-nine days. For if liberation is not achieved at one introduction, it can be achieved at another. This is the reason why, not just one, but many introductions should be given.

.   .   .

Then again, there are several kinds of persons who do not achieve liberation, despite having received the above introductions and having been taught the above visualization techniques. This lack of ability comes about through limited familiarity with virtuous past actions, extensive primal familiarity with nonvirtuous past actions, and the potency and great force of negative obscurations. So, at this stage, if the womb entrances have still not been successfully obstructed as described above, there is a profound oral instruction for choosing an appropriate womb entrance, which should now be presented. Again, one should request the assistance of the buddhas and bodhisattvas, take refuge in the Three Precious Jewels, and cultivate an altruistic intention. Then, as before, calling to the deceased by name, three times, one should say the following words:

. . .

O Child of Buddha Nature, (*repeat the name of the deceased*), listen carefully. Even though many authentic introductions to the instructions have previously been given to you, up until this stage you have not taken these to heart. Now, if you have been unable to obstruct the womb entrances, the time has actually come for you to assume a body. There are not just one, but several different kinds of profound and genuine instructions that relate to your choice of an appropriate womb entrance. So comprehend these well. Do not be distracted. Listen without distraction! Understand, and maintain a firm intention!

O Child of Buddha Nature, now, if you are to be born as a human, the indications and signs that relate to the environment into which you may be born, on one among the four continents, will arise. You must recognize these indications! Indeed, you must choose the continent based on a careful examination of these indications of the environment into which you may be born.

If you are to take birth on the Eastern Continent, Videha, you will see a lake, adorned by male and female swans. Do not be drawn toward this place! Call to mind the methods of reversal and apply these! For were you to go there, even though it is a happy and tranquil place, it is an environment where the sacred teachings do not flourish. So do not enter this continent!

If you are to take birth on the Southern Continent, Jambudvīpa, you will see grand and delightful mansions. If indeed you can enter here, do so!

If you are to take birth on the Western Continent, Apara-godanīya, you will see a lake adorned around its shores by male and female horses. Do not be drawn toward this place! Call to mind the methods of reversal and apply these! For even though it is a place of great wealth and abundant resources, it is an environment where the sacred teachings do not flourish. So do not enter this continent!

If you are to take birth on the Northern Continent, Uttara-kuru, you will see a lake adorned around its shores by cattle or a lake adorned by trees. Recognize these appearances as indications of the birth that you are about to assume! Do not enter there! For even though this is a place where there is longevity and which has merit, it is an environment where the sacred teachings do not flourish. So do not enter this continent!

If you are to take birth as a god you will see delightful celestial palaces, many-storied and composed of diverse jewels. If indeed you can, you should enter here!

If you are to take birth as an antigod, you will see exquisite groves and spinning wooden torches creating wheels of fire. Do not enter there, under any circumstances! Call to mind the methods of reversal and apply these!

If you are to take birth as an animal, you will see rocky caverns, empty hollows, and straw sheds, shrouded by mist. Do not enter there!

If you are to take birth as an anguished spirit, you will see tree-stumps, black protruding silhouettes, blind desolate gorges, or total darkness. Were you to go there, you would be born as an anguished spirit and experience the manifold sufferings of insatiable hunger and thirst. Do not enter there! Call to mind the methods of reversal and apply these! Be courageous and strong!

If you are to take birth as a hell being, you will hear the songs of those of negative past actions. Or, quite simply, you will feel powerless and compelled to enter. Whereupon, the perception will arise that you are moving into a land of darkness, where there are black and reddened houses, black earth-pits, and black roads. Were you to be drawn to this place, you would enter the hells and experience the searing unbearable sufferings of heat and cold. Be careful! Do not enter into the midst of this, for there will be no opportunity to turn back. Do not enter there, under any circumstances! As it is said in the root verses: "You must obstruct the womb entrances and call to mind the methods of reversal." These are wholly necessary now!

O Child of Buddha Nature, although you do not wish to move forward, you are powerless not to do so. The avenging forces, who are the executors of the unfailing laws of cause and effect, will be pursuing you. You will have no choice but to move forward. Before you, the avengers and executors will be leading the way. The experience will arise of trying to flee from these forces, of trying to flee from the darkness, from the most violent windstorms, from the thunderous tumult, the snow, the rain, the hail, and the turbulent blizzards, which swirl around you. Frightened, you will set off to seek a refuge and you will find protection inside an enclosed space, such as within the mansions, just described, or in rock-shelters, or holes in the ground, or among trees, or within the bud of a lotus flower. Hiding here, you will be very hesitant to come out, and you will think: "I should not leave here now." You will be very reluctant to be separated from this protected place and you will become utterly attached to it. Then, because you are so very hesitant to go outside, where you would be confronted by the fears and terrors of the intermediate state, you will, because of this fear and awe, continue to hide away. Thus, you will assume a body, however utterly bad that may be, and you will, in time, come to experience all manner of sufferings. This experience of wanting to hide is a sign that you are being obstructed by malignant forces and carnivorous ogres. Particularly related to this stage, there is a profound oral instruction. Listen, therefore, and understand!

At this time, when you are being pursued by avenging forces and you feel powerless to escape and you are terrified and frightened, you must, in an instant and with perfect recall, visualize the Transcendent Lord Mahottara Heruka, or Hayagrīva, or Vajrapāṇi, or else, if you have one, your personal meditational deity. Visualize the deity as having a huge buddha-body, with thick limbs, standing upright, in a terrifying wrathful manifestation, which pulverizes every form of obstructing force. By virtue of this practice, insulated from the avengers by the blessing and compassion of the meditational deity, you will secure the ability to choose a womb entrance. This is a profound and genuine crucial point of the oral instructions. So, understand this now!

Moreover, O Child of Buddha Nature, the gods inhabiting the form realms of meditative concentration, and similar beings of the higher realms, take birth through the potency of their meditative stability. Also, certain classes of malevolent forces, including the anguished spirits, arise on the basis of the transformation of their mental body itself during this very intermediate state, through a shift in their mode of perception. In this way, they assume the forms of an anguished spirit, malign force, or carnivorous ogre, capable of displaying diverse miraculous acts. The anguished spirits who reside in the ocean depths, the anguished spirits who move through space, the eighty thousand classes of obstructing forces, and so forth, all come into existence consequent on such a shift in their mode of perception, while still in the mental body.

At this time, therefore, while visualizing the wrathful deity, it is essential that you hold in mind the meaning of emptiness, the essence of the Great Seal. If you are not able to practice in this way, you must cultivate your experience of the illusion-like natural expressive power of actual reality. If you are unable even to practice in that way, you should meditate on the meditational deity Mahākāruṇika, without allowing your mind to experience attachment in any respect whatsoever. Through practicing this effectively, buddhahood will be attained in the Buddha-body of Perfect Resource during this intermediate state.

O Child of Buddha Nature, if, due to the potency of your past actions, you must at this stage enter a womb, a further teaching on the methods of choosing a womb entrance is now to be taught. Listen carefully, therefore! Do not just move toward whatever womb entrance appears to you. If, while being pursued by the avenging forces of the laws of cause and effect, you are powerless and unable to resist the process of entering a womb, then you must, at this time, meditate on Hayagrīva. Since you now possess a subtle, supernormal cognitive ability, you will clearly apprehend all the potential birthplaces as they arise, in sequence. Therefore, make your choice, based on the examination of the indications and based on the instructions! There are two kinds of oral instruction that can now be applied: first, the oral instructions for transferring the consciousness to the pure Buddha fields, and second, the instructions for choosing a womb entrance within impure cyclic existence. Therefore, listen carefully and do as follows:

First, the transference of consciousness to the utterly pure realms of the sky-farers is effected by those of highest ability, by directing their intention as follows. "Alas! I am deeply sad that even after an infinite 'incalculable aeon' I am still left behind in this swamp of cyclic existence. How dreadful it is, that while so many have attained buddhahood in the past, I have still not achieved liberation. Now, this cycle of existence disgusts me! It horrifies me! I have long been led astray by it! Now, the moment approaches for me to move forward! Now, I must take birth, miraculously, in the bud of a lotus flower, in the presence of the Buddha Amitābha, in the western Buddha field of The Blissful (*Sukhāvatī*)!" Focus your intention, concentratedly, on this thought! It is essential that you make this effort! Alternatively, you can focus your intention on whichever Buddha field you wish: on Manifest Joy (*Abhirati*), on Dense Array (*Ghanavyūha*), on Alakāvatī, on Mount Potālaka, or you may wish to focus on coming into the presence of Padmasambhava of Oḍḍiyāna, in the celestial palace of Lotus Light, or indeed on whichever Buddha field you wish to enter. Be single-minded! Do not be distracted! Immediately upon establishing this intention, you will take birth in the chosen Buddha field. Yet again, alternatively, if you wish to proceed into the presence of Maitreya in the realm of The Joyful

(*Tuṣita*), think as follows: "At this juncture in the intermediate state, the moment has come for me to proceed into the presence of the king of the sacred teachings, Maitreya, in the realm of The Joyful. Therefore, it is there that I will go!" If you focus your intention on this thought, you will take birth, miraculously, in the heart of a lotus, in the presence of Maitreya.

Alternatively, if you are unable to accomplish this transference, or if you desire to enter a womb or you are obliged to enter one, then there are the following instructions on choosing a womb entrance within impure cyclic existence. Therefore, listen carefully. Utilizing the supernormal cognitive ability you now possess, examine the continents once again, as just described, and make your choice. You must enter a land where the sacred teachings flourish!

Be warned, however! It could be that, in reality, you are about to take birth by entering into a substance that is fetid and polluted, and yet that filthy mass will be perceived by you as sweet-smelling and you will be drawn toward it and take birth within it. Therefore, whatever such attractive appearances may arise, do not grasp at them as substantially real! Ensure that you remain utterly free from the symptoms of attachment and aversion, and on that basis choose an excellent womb entrance.

It is extremely important that your motivation be firmly concentrated as you approach the womb entrance. Therefore think as follows: "Ah! For the sake of all sentient beings, I shall be born as a universal monarch, or acting purely like a great dignified sal tree, I shall be born into the brāhman class, or as the child of an accomplished master, or into a family that maintains an immaculate lineage of the sacred teachings, or into a family where the mother and father are deeply devout. Then, once I have taken on a body that is blessed with the merit of being able to act on behalf of all sentient beings, I shall dedicate myself to acting on their behalf!" You must concentrate your motivation on this thought and thus enter the womb.

As you enter the womb, consecrate it by perceiving it as a celestial palace of the deities. Be full of devotion. Ensure that you enter while praying to and imagining that you are receiving empowerments from the conquerors of the ten directions and from their sons, as well as from the meditational deities and, in particular, from Mahākāruṇika.

However, be warned, for as you make this choice of a womb entrance, there is a risk of error. There is the risk of error when, through the potency of past actions, an excellent womb entrance is perceived as a bad one, and when a bad womb entrance is perceived as a good one. At this time, the essential points of the teaching are crucial. Therefore, once again, you should act as follows. Even though perceptions of an excellent womb entrance may occur, do not become attached to these. And conversely, even though perceptions of a poor womb entrance may occur, do not feel aversion. The essential point of the profound and genuine instructions is that you enter the womb in a state of great equanimity, utterly free from the dichotomies of good and bad, acceptance and rejection, or attachment and aversion.

· · ·

Nevertheless, with the exception of certain persons who have experience of this equanimity, it is difficult for beings to sever themselves from the deep-seated and long-lasting disease of negative habitual tendencies. Therefore, if the deceased remains unable to be free from attachment and aversion, in the above manner, such negative beings who are of the lowest capacity may seek refuge in the animal realms or similar kinds of inferior existences. In order to counteract this, again calling to the deceased by name, you should speak as follows:

．　　　．　　　．

O Child of Buddha Nature, if you do not know how to choose a womb entrance and you are unable to give up your attachment and your aversion, then, regardless of which of the above appearances arise, you must call out, by name, to the Three Precious Jewels. Take refuge in them! Pray to Mahākāruṇika! Go forward with your head held high. Recognize that this is the intermediate state! Give up your attachment and your clinging to the friends, sons, daughters, and relatives that you have left behind. These attachments are not helpful to you now. Enter into the blue light of the human realm. Enter into the white light of the realm of the gods. Enter into the mansions of precious jewels and the gardens of delight.

CONCLUSION

It would be extremely beneficial if this sacred teaching of the "Great Liberation by Hearing in the Intermediate States" was recited as a complement to other systems of meditative guidance, irrespective of the category of the sacred teachings to which they belong.

Further, this text should be recited constantly. Its words and meaning should be learned by heart. Then, if one's health permits, when the onset of the intermediate state of the time of death becomes certain, and the signs of approaching death are recognized, one should read this text aloud to oneself, and reflect on its words and meaning. If one's health does not allow this, then entrust the book to a fellow Buddhist for him or her to read aloud. The reminder thus being made, there is no doubt that liberation will assuredly be attained.

This teaching, which does not necessarily require prior meditation practice, is the profound instruction that liberates by being seen, liberates by being heard, and liberates by being read aloud. This profound instruction is one that can lead even those of the greatest negativity on the direct path to liberation. Ensure that its words and meaning are retained in the memory such that they are not forgotten, even if you were to be chased by seven ferocious dogs. This is a pith instruction for the attainment of buddhahood at the time of death. Even if all the buddhas of the past, present, and future were to search, they would not find a sacred teaching superior to this.

This completes the instruction on the intermediate state, which liberates corporeal beings, the profound, refined essence entitled the "Great Liberation by Hearing in the Intermediate States." It was brought forth from the mountain of Gampodar by the accomplished master Karma Lingpa, as a precious treasure.

Glossary of Key Terms

aggregate *phung-po*, Skt. *skandha* A general philosophical term refer-
ring to the principal psycho-physical components that constitute the
mind-body complex of a person. Buddhist literature speaks of five such
components, technically known as the five psycho-physical aggregates.
These are the aggregate of form, the aggregate of feelings, the aggregate
of perceptions, the aggregate of motivational tendencies, and the aggregate of consciousness. See individual entries below.

aggregate of consciousness *rnam-par shes-pa'i phung-po*, Skt.
vijñānaskandha In the context of our text the aggregate of consciousness comprises the so-called "eight classes of consciousness."
These are: 1) the ground-of-all consciousness, which is an undifferentiated
foundational consciousness underlying all the other aspects of consciousness and in which are stored the imprints left by past experiences;
2) the deluded consciousness, which is pervaded by fundamental ignorance and is responsible for our sense of selfhood and dualistic misapprehension of the true nature of phenomena; 3) the mental consciousness,

which objectively refers to mental constructs, thoughts, and the experience of our senses; 4) visual consciousness; 5) auditory consciousness; 6) olfactory consciousness; 7) gustatory consciousness; and 8) tactile consciousness.

aggregate of feelings *tshor-ba'i phung-po*, Skt. *vedanāskandha* The aggregate of feelings encompasses the pleasant, unpleasant, and neutral sensations that arise as an immediate reaction to the objects of our senses.

aggregate of form *gzugs-kyi phung-po*, Skt. *rūpaskandha* The aggregate of form includes both the subtle and manifest forms derived from the elements and experienced through the five senses, including, of course, our bodies and the environment. The aggregate of form is considered to have fifteen aspects, namely those related to the elements (earth, water, fire, and wind); those related to the five sense objects (visual forms, sounds, smells, tastes, and contacts); those related to the five sense organs (eye, ear, nose, tongue, and body); and, lastly, that aspect related to imperceptible forms, which are said to be continuously present throughout past, present, and future time.

aggregate of motivational tendencies *'du-byas-kyi phung-po*, Skt. *saṃskāraskandha* The aggregate of motivational tendencies refers to the array of specific types of causative mental states that give rise to our characteristic perspectives and emotions and which in turn condition our actions.

aggregate of perceptions *'du-shes-kyi phung-po*, Skt. *saṃjñāskandha* The aggregate of perceptions recognizes and identifies forms and objects. It differentiates one form or object from another and names them.

anguished spirits *yi-dvags*, Skt. *preta* Among the six classes of living beings, the anguished spirits are characterized as being in a state of existence that, in terms of the degree of suffering, is intermediate to the animal and hell realms. Born as a result of a preponderance of miserliness and unfulfilled self-centered ambition in their past actions, they are characterized by unsatisfied craving.

antigod *lha-ma-yin*, Skt. *asura* One of six classes of living beings. The mode of being and activity of the antigods is said to be engendered and dominated by envy, self-centered ambition, and hostility. They are metaphorically described as being incessantly embroiled in a dispute with the gods over the possession of a magical tree.

auspicious aeon *bskal-pa bzang-po*, Skt. *bhadrakalpa* The name of the present aeon of time, during which one thousand buddhas are predicted to appear in succession. Among these, *Śākyamuni Buddha* is regarded as the fourth and *Maitreya* as the fifth.

Avalokiteśvara *spyan-ras gzigs dbang-phyug Avalokiteśvara* is regarded as the embodiment of the compassionate aspect of the mind of all the buddhas, manifesting in the form of a meditational deity. He is revered as the patron deity of Tibet and has many different aspects, the most popular including the seated four-armed white form and "thousand-armed" form *Mahākāruṇika*.

aversion *zhe-sdang*, Skt. *dveṣa* In Buddhist literature, the terms aversion and hatred are often used interchangeably with anger. In its subtle manifestation, aversion is said to obstruct an individual from a correct perception of forms. In its extreme manifestation, as overwhelming hatred and fear, it is said to be characteristic of the worlds of the hells.

awareness *rig-pa*, Skt. *vidyā* As an ordinary verb, the Tibetan term *rig-pa* means "to know" or "to be aware." When used as a noun, it has several distinct though not unrelated meanings, corresponding to the Sanskrit *vidyā*: 1) as a general term encompassing all experiences of consciousness and mental events; 2) as intelligence or mental aptitude; 3) as a science or knowledge-based discipline; and 4) as a pure awareness. Our text generally assumes the last of these meanings, in which case it is a synonym or abbreviation for intrinsic awareness. See **intrinsic awareness**.

awareness holder *rig-'dzin*, Skt. *vidyādhara* The awareness holders or knowledge holders are embodiments of the great accomplished masters who have attained the highest realizations of the *tantras*.

blessing *byin-rlabs*, Skt. *adhiṣṭhāna* In the Buddhist context, the term *blessing* should not be understood in terms of grace as in the case of theistic religions. Rather, it relates to the sense of inspiration received from an external source, which transforms or awakens the potentials inherent within an individual's mental continuum. Thus, the Tibetan word *byin-rlabs* is interpreted to mean "to be transformed through inspiring magnificence."

bodhisattva *byang-chub sems-dpa'* A spiritual trainee dedicated to the cultivation and fulfillment of the altruistic intention to attain enlightenment. An essential element of this commitment to work for others is the determination purposely to remain within cyclic existence instead of simply seeking freedom from suffering for oneself. Philosophically, the *bodhisattva* is said to have fully realized the two aspects of selflessness, with respect to dissonant mental states and the nature of all phenomena.

buddha *sangs-rgyas* The Sanskrit term *buddha* literally means "awakened," "developed," or "enlightened." The Tibetan equivalent *sangs-rgyas* is a combination of *sangs-pa* ("awakened" or "purified") and *rgyas-pa* ("developed"). These two words in this context denote a full awakening from fundamental ignorance and a full realization of true knowledge (i.e., the pristine cognition of buddha-mind). A fully awakened being is therefore one who, as a result of training the mind through the *bodhisattva* paths, has finally realized his or her full potential for complete enlightenment, and has eliminated all the obscurations to true knowledge and liberation.

buddha-body *sku*, Skt. *kāya* The term *buddha-body* refers not only to the physical body of a buddha, but also to the varying "dimensions" in which the embodiment of fully enlightened attributes is present. See individual entries below.

Buddha-body of Emanation *sprul-sku*, Skt. *nirmāṇakāya* The Buddha-body of Emanation is the visible, and usually physical, manifestation of fully enlightened beings that arises spontaneously from the expanse of the Buddha-body of Reality, whenever appropriate, in accordance with the diverse dispositions of sentient beings.

Buddha-body of Perfect Resource *longs-spyod rdzogs-pa'i sku*, Skt. *sambhogakāya* The Buddha-body of Perfect Resource refers to the luminous, immaterial, and unimpeded reflection-like forms of the pure energy of enlightened mind, which become spontaneously present and naturally manifest at very high levels of realization—that is to say at the point at which the duality between subject and object dissolves. The intermediate state of reality is considered to be an optimum time for the realization of the Buddha-body of Perfect Resource.

Buddha-body of Reality *chos-sku*, Skt. *dharmakāya* The Buddha-body of Reality is the ultimate nature or essence of the enlightened mind, which is uncreated, free from the limits of conceptual elaboration, empty of inherent existence, naturally radiant, beyond duality, and spacious like the sky. The intermediate state of the time of death is considered to be an optimum time for the realization of the Buddha-body of Reality.

Buddha family *de-bzhin gshegs-pa'i rigs*, Skt. *tathāgatakula* One of the five families into which the meditational deities of the Buddha-body of Perfect Resource are subdivided.

Buddha field *zhings-khams*, Skt. *[buddha]kṣetra* The operational fields or "paradises" presided over by specific buddhas, which spontaneously arise as a result of their altruistic aspirations, are known as Buddha fields. Such environments are totally free from suffering, both physical and mental, and they transcend the mundane god realms inhabited by sentient beings of the world-systems of desire, form, and formlessness. It is said that when sentient beings, who have not yet been permanently released from the bondage of cyclic existence, have an affinity with a specific buddha and are consequently born into a respective pure realm, they do become temporarily free not only from manifest sufferings of the body and mind but also from the pervasive sufferings of past conditioning. Such fields or pure realms are regarded as conducive to the continuing cultivation of the path to buddhahood.

buddhahood *sangs-rgyas nyid / sangs-rgyas-kyi go-phang*, Skt. *buddhatva/ buddhapada* The attainment of a buddha, who has not only gained total freedom from karmically conditioned existence and overcome all the tendencies imprinted on the mind as a result of a long association with dissonant mental states, but also fully realized or manifested all aspects of buddha-body, buddha-speech, buddha-mind, buddha-attributes, and buddha-activities.

buddha-mind *thugs*, Skt. *citta* The term *buddha-mind* is synonymous with pristine cognition, five modes of which are differentiated. See **pristine cognition**.

Buddha nature *rigs*, Skt. *gotra* The seed of enlightenment inherent within the mental continuum of all sentient beings. It is this potential that makes it possible for every individual to realize the ultimate nature, given the application of appropriate methods. The notion of buddha nature is intimately linked with the Buddhist concept of the essential nature of mind, which according to Buddhism is considered to be pure, knowing, and luminous. Dissonant mental states such as attachment, aversion, and jealousy, which perpetually afflict our mind and give rise to suffering, are not the essential elements of our mind but adventitious and conditioned tendencies. Moreover, these dissonant states are all rooted in an ignorant state of mind that misapprehends the true nature of reality. Hence, through gaining genuine insights into the true nature of reality, misconceptions can be dispelled, thus cutting the root of all our dissonant mental states and allowing the Buddha nature within to manifest.

calm abiding *zhi-gnas*, Skt. *śamatha* Calm abiding is a meditative technique common to the entire Buddhist tradition, characterized by a stabilization of attention on an internal object of observation conjoined with the calming of external distractions to the mind. Calm abiding is an essential basis for training one's mind in the generation of penetrative insight, a true analytical insight into the more profound aspects of a chosen object, such as its emptiness or ultimate nature.

cause and effect *rgyu-'bras*, Skt. *hetuphala* In the context of Buddhist philosophy the term refers to the natural law that exists between a cause and its effect. Some of the principal features of the law are: 1) nothing evolves uncaused; 2) any entity that itself lacks a process of change cannot cause any other event; and 3) only causes that possess natures that accord with specific effects can lead to those effects. The term "cause and effect" is often used to translate the Sanskrit word *karma*, which literally means "action." See **past actions**.

celestial palace *gzhal-yas-khang*, Skt. *vimāna* See **maṇḍala**.

central channel *rtsa dbu-ma*, Skt. *avadhūti* See **energy channels**.

channel branch *rtsa-'dab* According to the *tantras* and related medical traditions, there are five energy centers located along the central channel of the body at the focal points of the crown, throat, heart, navel, and genitalia. A specific number of channel branches emerge from each of these energy centers, and these in turn conduct vital energy throughout the body through a network of 72,000 minor channels. See **energy channels**.

chiliocosm *stong dang-po 'jig-rten-gyi khams*, Skt. *sahasralokadhātu* According to traditional Indian Buddhist cosmology, the world of the four continents surrounding Mount Sumeru when multiplied one thousand times forms a chiliocosm of parallel worlds.

cīvaṃcīvaka *shang-shang* A mythical creature with the head, arms, and torso of a human being and the wings and legs of a bird.

compassion *snying-rje/thugs-rje*, Skt. *karuṇā* In Buddhist literature, the term *compassion* is often used as a synonym for "great compassion" (*mahākaruṇā*), which refers to a totally unbiased mind that aspires to the liberation of all sentient beings from suffering, equally. Compassion is said to become "great" only when, through proper training of the mind, such an altruistic aspiration becomes spontaneous and no longer requires any conscious effort for its arising. The measure of having realized such a state is that one spontaneously feels a sense of intimacy and compassion toward all others, with the same degree of commitment and intensity that one feels toward one's most beloved. It is worth bearing in mind that in Buddhism compassion should not be understood in terms of pity, which may imply a feeling of superiority toward the object of compassion.

conqueror *rgyal-ba*, Skt. *jina* In Buddhist literature, this term is an epithet for a buddha.

consciousness *rnam-par shes-pa*, Skt. *vijñāna* In Buddhism, consciousness is defined as "an awareness that is knowing and luminous." It is not physical and thus lacks any resistance to obstruction. It has neither shape nor color; it can be experienced but not externally perceived as an object. In short, it includes both the conscious cognitive events and the subconscious aspects of the mind through which we know and perceive the world, as well as the emotions. A distinction is made between the mundane consciousness of sentient beings and the pristine cognition of the buddhas. See **pristine cognition** and **aggregate of consciousness**.

consciousness transference *'pho-ba*, Skt. *saṃkrānti* A unique tantric practice undertaken to transfer the consciousness at the time of death, ideally to the unconditioned state of the realization of the Buddha-body of Reality, or to a realm of existence with a favorable migration, ideally the pure realm of a meditational deity. Practitioners must train thoroughly in advance before actually performing the transference of consciousness at the time of death, whether on one's own behalf or on behalf of another.

cyclic existence *'khor-ba*, Skt. *saṃsāra* A state of existence conditioned by dissonant mental states and the imprint of past actions (*karma*), characterized by suffering in a cycle of life, death, and rebirth, in which the six classes of sentient beings rotate. Cyclic existence emerges from fundamental ignorance through a process known as the twelve links of dependent origination. When fundamental ignorance, identified as the misapprehension of the nature of actual reality, is reversed, cyclic existence is itself reversed and the contrasting state of *nirvāṇa* is attained, free from suffering and the processes of rebirth. See **dependent origination** and **nirvāṇa**.

Dalai Lama *rgyal ba yid-bzhin nor-bu/rin-po-che* The temporal and spiritual leader of Tibet. The Dalai Lama's temporal reign began at the time of the fifth Dalai Lama in the seventeenth century. Since then the country has been ruled, periodically, by a succession of Dalai Lamas, until China's occupation in the 1950s. The Dalai Lamas are chosen according to a strict traditional procedure of observation and examination initiated following the death of the previous Dalai Lama. The present Dalai Lama is the fourteenth in the succession of this lineage. The title Dalai Lama was originally offered to Sonam Gyatso, the third Dalai Lama, by the then Mongol prince Altan Qan. The Mongol word *dalai, gyatso* in Tibetan, means "ocean (of wisdom)."

deity *yi-dam*, Skt. *iṣṭadevatā* See under **meditational deity**.

delusion *gti-mug*, Skt. *moha* Delusion is the obfuscating mental factor that obstructs an individual from generating knowledge or insight.

dependent origination *rten-'brel*, Skt. *pratītyasamutpāda* The doctrine of dependent origination can be said to be the most fundamental metaphysical view of Buddhist thought and it is intimately linked with the Buddhist notion of causation. The principle of dependent origination asserts that nothing exists independently of other factors, the reason for this being that things and events come into existence only by dependence on the aggregation of multiple causes and conditions. In general, the processes of cyclic existence, through which the external world and the sentient beings within it revolve in a continuous cycle of suffering (propelled by the propensities of past actions and their interaction with dissonant mental states), are said to originate through dependence on twelve successive links, which are known as the twelve links of dependent origination. These comprise: 1) fundamental ignorance, 2) motivational tendencies, 3) consciousness, 4) name and form, 5) sensory activity fields, 6) contact, 7) sensation, 8) attachment, 9) grasping, 10) rebirth process, 11) birth, 12) aging and death. Although in the ultimate sense there is no beginning to the continuum of mind, a relative beginning can be spoken of on the basis of a single instance of rebirth within cyclic existence. Every instance of birth in cyclic existence must have a cause and such causes are ultimately rooted in our fundamental ignorance, which misapprehends the true nature of actual reality. For an ordinary sentient being, all the twelve links are interconnected and each component of the chain contributes to the perpetuation of the cycle. It is only through deliberate reversal of fundamental ignorance that one can succeed in bringing the whole cycle to an end. Fundamental ignorance gives rise to conditioning or tendencies that are stored in the substratum or ground-of-all consciousness. Following the moment of a sentient being's conception, this inheritance of past actions from a previous life gives rise to name and form, i.e. to the five psycho-physical aggregates, which are products of that dualizing consciousness. Then, the sensory activity fields provide the subjective and objective framework for sensory activity in its initial stages of development, while contact refers to the maturation of sensory perception as an unborn child develops a sensitivity to its environment inside the womb. Thereafter, sensation, attachment, grasping, rebirth process, and actual birth together indicate the emergence of a sentient being within the living world, and these in turn lead inevitably to old age and death.

discriminative awareness *shes-rab*, Skt. *prajñā* The Sanskrit term *prajñā* can be formally defined as "the discriminative awareness of the essence, distinctions, particular and general characteristics, and advantages and disadvantages of any object within one's own perceptual range, at the conclusion of which doubts are removed." In other words, this is the faculty of intelligence or discriminating awareness inherent within the mental continuum of all living creatures that enables them to examine the characteristics of things and events, thus making it possible to make judgments and deliberations.

dissonant mental states *nyon-mongs*, Skt. *kleśa* The essentially pure nature of mind is obscured and afflicted by the various psychological defilements known as the dissonant mental states. The Tibetan word *nyon-mong* implies a mental event whose arising causes psychological afflictions within the mind, thus destroying its peace and composure. According to classical Buddhist literature, there are six primary dissonant mental states: fundamental ignorance, attachment, aversion, pride, doubt, and afflicted or dissonant views; and an enumeration of twenty subsidiary mental states that comprise: anger, malice, dissimulation, fury, envy, miserliness, dishonesty, deception, arrogance, mischief, indecorum, indecency, obfuscation, agitation, distrust, laziness, carelessness, forgetfulness, distraction, and inattentiveness. Even more wide-ranging are the 84,000 dissonant mental states for which the 84,000 aspects of the sacred teachings are said to provide distinctive antidotes. At the root of all these psychological afflictions lies the fundamental ignorance that misapprehends the true nature of reality.

Dzogchen *rdzogs-chen*, Skt. *mahāsandhi* See **Great Perfection**.

elements and **elemental properties** *'byung ba*, Skt. *bhūta* See **five elements**.

empowerment *dbang-bskur*, Skt. *abhiṣeka* A ritual ceremony performed by accomplished spiritual teachers and lineage holders to empower prospective trainees prior to their engaging in the various vehicles and specific practices of the *tantras*. The meditative processes of the empowerment ritual are intended to activate the potentials inherent within the body, speech, and mind of the trainee—in other words to awaken the seed of the natural ability to engage in the practice. Such empowerment ceremonies are an essential prerequisite for the practice of *tantra* in the Buddhist tradition.

emptiness *stong-pa-nyid*, Skt. *śūnyatā* The ultimate nature of reality. The theory of emptiness is most systematically developed in the writings of the second-century Buddhist thinker Nāgārjuna, the founder of the *Madhyamaka* or Middle Way school. According to this view, all things and events, both external and internal, are devoid of any independent, intrinsic reality that constitutes their essence. Nothing can be said to exist independently from the complex network of factors that gives rise to its origination, nor are phenomena independent of the cognitive processes and conceptual designations (mental constructs) that make up the conventional framework within which their identity and existence are posited. It is our deeply ingrained tendency to conceive of things as materially existing in their own right that conditions and compels us to perceive and grasp at a substantial reality of things and our own existence. In turn, when all levels of conceptualization dissolve and when all forms of dichotomizing tendencies are quelled through deliberate meditative deconstruction of conceptual elaborations, Nāgārjuna argues, the ultimate nature of reality—emptiness—will finally become manifest.

energy center *rtsa-'khor*, Skt. *cakra* According to the *tantras* and related medical traditions, there are five energy centers within the subtle body. These are located at the crown, throat, heart, navel, and genitalia, where the right and left channels are said to loop around the central channel, forming knots that obstruct the flow of subtle energy into the central channel. At each of the five energy centers there are a diverse number of channel branches through which vital energy is conducted throughout the body.

energy channels *rtsa*, Skt. *nāḍī* In the *tantras* and related medical traditions, it is said that there are 72,000 veinlike channels through which flow the vital energies or subtle winds that sustain life and which also give rise to various conceptual states within the individual's mind. Three main channels run vertically from the crown fontanelle of the head down to the genitalia, intersecting at the five energy centers of the crown, throat, heart, navel, and genitalia. All the minor energy channels branch off from these energy centers to permeate the body.

enlightened intention *dgongs-pa*, Skt. *abhiprāya* In the context of our text, enlightened intention refers to the unimpeded, nonconceptual, and compassionate intention of the buddhas.

enlightenment *byang-chub*, Skt. *bodhi* In the Buddhist context, *enlightenment* refers to an individual's awakening to the mind's actual nature.

envy *phrag-dog*, Skt. *īrṣā* In Buddhist literature envy includes all the various forms of self-cherishing ambition. In its extreme manifestation— persistent hostile competitiveness—it is said to characterize the worlds of the antigods.

five elements *'byung-ba lnga / khams lnga*, Skt. *pañcabhūta/pañcadhātu* According to the Indo-Tibetan system, as expounded in the *tantras* and in medical and astrological texts, the five elements—earth, water, fire, wind, and space—are basic components that make up our environment, our bodies, and, at their subtle levels, modalities of the mind. At the subtlest level, the elemental properties exist as the pure natures represented by the five female buddhas (*Ākāśadhātvīśvarī, Buddhalocanā, Māmakī, Pāṇḍaravāsinī,* and *Samayatārā*) and these manifest as the physical properties of earth (solidity), water (fluidity), fire (heat and light), wind (movement and energy), and space—in other words as all the qualities that constitute the physical forms we experience through our senses. A proper understanding of the elements and the way in which their properties permeate the nature of mind, the body, and our environment is fundamental to the practice of Buddhist *tantra*.

form realm and **formless realm** See **three world-systems**.

four continents and eight subcontinents *gling bzhi-dang gling-phran brgyad* According to traditional Indian Buddhist cosmology, the world has Mount Sumeru as its central axis, surrounded by seven concentric oceans divided from one another by seven successive ranges of golden mountains. The entire world is girded by a perimeter of iron mountains.

In each of the four cardinal directions of Mount Sumeru there is located a continent, along with two satellites or subcontinents. Among the four continents, *Jambudvīpa*, in the south, is unique in that it is here that the sacred teachings of the buddhas are said to flourish.

fundamental ignorance *ma-rig-pa*, Skt. *avidyā* The most fundamental misapprehension of the nature of actual reality, which is the source of all dissonant mental states and the twelve links of dependent origination. See **dependent origination** and **dissonant mental states**.

generation stage *bskyed-rim*, Skt. *utpattikrama* According to the traditions of the *tantras*, the main practices of meditation that follow the successful conclusion of the preliminary practices include the generation stage and the perfection stage. Both the generation and perfection stages of meditation are related to transforming our mundane experiences of each of the phases of life and death, namely: the intermediate states of the time of death, of reality, of rebirth, and of living. The generation stage is characterized by the meditative processes of the practitioner's gradual identification with the form and pristine cognition of the meditational deity and it is during this stage that, with the support of *mantra* recitation, the elaborate visualization of the deity is gradually generated and stabilized. This process, known as self-generation, is a simulacrum of bringing the three buddha-bodies on to the path and is composed therefore of three principal aspects: dissolution into emptiness (Buddha-body of Reality), arising into a subtle form such as a seed syllable or symbol (Buddha-body of Perfect Resource), and full emergence into the deity's form (Buddha-body of Emanation). See **perfection stage**.

gods *lha*, Skt. *deva* One of the six classes of living beings. The mode of being and activity of the gods is said to be engendered and dominated by exaltation, indulgence, and pride. The gods exist in realms higher than that of the human realm in the world-system of desire, and also in the world-systems of form and formlessness. See **three world-systems**.

Great Perfection *rdzogs-pa chen-po*, Skt. *mahasandhi* Great Perfection is a synonym for *atiyoga*, the highest teaching and meditative practice of the oldest school of Tibetan Buddhism (*Nyingma*).

Great Seal *phyag-rgya chen-po*, Skt. *mahāmudrā* In a general sense, the expression Great Seal refers to the comprehension of emptiness as the all-encompassing ultimate nature of reality. More specifically it refers to a systematic series of advanced meditations focusing on the meditator's own mind. See **emptiness**.

ground-of-all consciousness *kun-gzhi'i rnam-par shes-pa*, Skt. *ālaya-vijñāna* See **aggregate of consciousness**.

habitual tendencies *bag-chags*, Skt. *vāsanā* The deep-seated propensities and habitual tendencies inherited from our past actions. This concept of habitual tendencies is critical to the Buddhist understanding of the causal dynamics of karmic actions as well as its understanding of the process of conditioning. For example, when a person commits an act, such as the negative act of killing, the act itself does not last. So that which connects the commitment of this act and the experiencing of its future consequence, in some instances in a future life, is the habitual tendencies imprinted upon one's psyche by the act committed. Similarly, when a strong emotion such as a feeling of hatred arises, although the actual emotion may subside after a while, the experience leaves a mark or an imprint, which will continue to have an impact on the person's attitudes, emotions, and behavior. It is the collection of such countless habitual tendencies imprinted on our psyche by dissonant mental states that constitutes the obscurations and misconceptions concerning the known range of phenomena, the total eradication of which occurs only when one achieves full awakening or buddhahood. See **obscuration**.

Hayagrīva *rta-mgrin Hayagrīva* is a wrathful form of the meditational deity *Avalokiteśvara*. See **Avalokiteśvara** and **wrath**.

Highest Yoga Tantra *bla-med rgyud*, Skt. *Yoganiruttaratantra* The highest among the four classes of *tantra*, the other three being: *Kriyā*, *Caryā*, and *Yoga tantra*. The differences between the four classes of *tantra* represent stages of ever-decreasing emphasis on external ritual and ever-increasing subtlety of internal meditation. *Niruttara* means "unsurpassed" or "highest" and it is in the *Yoganiruttara tantras* that the meditative techniques for realizing the three buddha-bodies are the most subtle and refined.

ignorance *ma-rig-pa*, Skt. *avidyā* See **fundamental ignorance**.

impermanence *mi-rtag-pa*, Skt. *anitya* Impermanence, along with suffering and the absence of self-identity, is regarded in Buddhism as one of the three marks or characteristics of causally conditioned phenomena. Although Buddhist literature mentions various degrees of impermanence, in general it can be defined as the moment-by-moment changing nature of all things. Nothing endures through time without change, and the process of change is dynamic and never-ending, reflecting the nature of flux and fluidity in conditioned existence. This fundamental quality of impermanence extends to both the external world and the perceiving mind.

inherent existence *rang-ngo-bo-nyid*, Skt. *svabhāvatā* The term *inherent existence* refers to the ontological status of phenomena, according to which phenomena are attributed with existence in their own right, inherently, in and of themselves, objectively, and independent of any other phenomena such as our conception and labeling. The *Madhyamaka* or Middle Way schools of thought refute such a nature of existence and argue that nothing exists inherently, for ultimately nothing can be found to exist independent of conceptuality and labeling. The

Madhyamaka schools hold that things exist only conventionally and their existence can be validated only within a relative framework of conventional reality. Absence of such an ontological reality, i.e. the absence of the inherent existence of all phenomena, is defined as the true nature of reality—emptiness—by the *Madhyamaka* schools and by the *tantras*.

inner radiance *'od-gsal*, Skt. *prabhāsvara* Sometimes also translated as "clear light," the Tibetan term *'od-gsal*, which has been rendered here as "inner radiance," refers in the context of the perfection stage of meditation to the subtlest level of mind, i.e. the fundamental, essential nature of all our cognitive events. Though ever present within all sentient beings, this inner radiance becomes manifest only when the gross mind has ceased to function. Such a dissolution is experienced by ordinary beings, naturally, at the time of death, but it can also be experientially cultivated through the practices of Highest Yoga Tantra. A fundamental distinction is made between the inner radiance of the ground and the inner radiance of the path. The former, which is also known as "the mother inner radiance," occurs naturally at the time of death, when it indicates the presence of the Buddha-body of Reality, but which may not be accompanied by an awareness of its nature. The latter, which is also known as "the child inner radiance," is an awareness of the ultimate nature of mind cultivated by the meditator in life, i.e. the realization of the nature of the mother inner radiance as it is developed in meditation. Buddhahood is achieved when the mother inner radiance and child inner radiance conjoin.

intermediate state *bar-do*, Skt. *antarābhava* The original usage of the term within classical Buddhist literature suggests that it referred exclusively to the period between the time of death and the time of rebirth. In the context of our text, however, the term *intermediate state* refers also to key phases of life and death identified as: the intermediate state of living, the intermediate state of meditative concentration, the intermediate state of dreams, the intermediate state of the time of death, the intermediate state of reality, and the intermediate state of rebirth. During each of these phases, the consciousness of a person has particular experiential qualities, and corresponding to these qualities of experience there are specific meditative techniques conducive to realization of the ultimate nature of mind and phenomena. See individual entries below.

intermediate state of dreams *rmi-lam bar-do* The intermediate state of dreams begins from the moment of falling asleep and ends when we wake. This intermediate state offers the opportunity for the practitioner to recognize the similarity between the illusory nature of dreams and that of our waking state. This practice is cultivated in the context of dream yoga where the ability to maintain awareness of the ultimate nature of mind and phenomena during both deep sleep and dreaming is refined.

intermediate state of living *rang-bzhin bar-do* The intermediate state of living begins at the time of birth and continues until the time of death. Having obtained a precious human form with the ability to recognize our actual condition, the opportunity arises to adopt a way of life and to engage in the practices that lead to buddhahood.

intermediate state of meditative concentration *bsam-gtan bar-do* The intermediate state of meditative concentration entered during the waking state provides the opportunity for the practitioner to cultivate meditative equipoise (*samāhita*) and thereby to achieve stability in the generation and perfection stages of meditation. This in turn deepens an unbroken awareness of the ultimate nature of mind and phenomena in postmeditative activities and prepares the meditator for the intermediate state of the time of death.

intermediate state of reality *chos-nyid bar-do* The intermediate state of actual reality arises after the intermediate state of the time of death and before the intermediate state of rebirth. Here the opportunity occurs, based on the practices adopted during one's lifetime, to recognize the natural purity and natural transformative qualities of the ultimate nature of mind in the form of luminosities, rays, sounds, and meditational deities.

intermediate state of rebirth *srid-pa'i bar-do* The intermediate state of rebirth is entered after the intermediate state of reality when the consciousness arises in the form of a mental body, conditioned by the individual's inheritance of past actions, and the individual begins to experience both the surroundings where they died and the unfolding of experiential states driven by the momentum of past actions. If liberation from cyclic existence is not achieved during this intermediate state, it comes to an end at the moment of conception. Since consciousness is said to possess certain heightened qualities during this period, there is a potential to achieve liberation, or at the very least a favorable rebirth, at various key stages as this state is traversed.

intermediate state of the time of death *'chi-kha'i bar-do* The intermediate state of the time of death is entered at the time when the process of dying definitively begins and ends with the onset of the intermediate state of reality. It includes the gradual dissolution of the five elements and their associated modes of consciousness, and culminates with the arising of the inner radiance of the ground. The natural arising of inner radiance immediately after respiration ceases is regarded as a supreme opportunity to realize the Buddha-body of Reality.

intrinsic awareness *rang-rig*, Skt. *svasaṃvitti/svasaṃvedana* In the context of the present work, intrinsic awareness refers to the underlying, fundamental nature of mind in its natural state of spontaneity and purity, beyond the subject-object dichotomy. As such, intrinsic awareness gives the meditator access to pristine cognition or the buddha-mind itself.

Kaṅkaṇīdhāraṇī *kaṅ-ka-ṇī gzungs* The name of an incantation text through which offerings are made on behalf of the deceased.

karma *las* See **past actions**.

Karma family *las-kyi rigs*, Skt. *karmakula* One of the five families into which the meditational deities of the Buddha-body of Perfect Resource are subdivided.

liberation *grol-ba/sgrol-ba*, Skt. *mokṣa* In a Buddhist context, the term *liberation* refers specifically to freedom from cyclic existence, the karmically conditioned cycle of death and rebirth, and consequently to freedom from all forms of physical and mental suffering. Such a liberation can be attained only through the total elimination of fundamental ignorance and the dissonant mental states, including attachment and aversion, which afflict the mind and perpetuate the cycle of existence.

lineage *brgyud-pa*, Skt. *paramparā* An unbroken line of successive teachers through whom the Buddhist teachings are transmitted.

lineage holder *brgyud-pa'i 'dzin-pa*, Skt. *paramparādhara* One who maintains any of the lineages of Buddhist teachings and takes responsibility for their continued transmission from one generation to the next. See previous entry.

lotus *padma* In Buddhist poetry and the visual arts, the lotus, particularly the variety that grows in water, is often used as a symbol of purity. The lotus grows from an unclean mire, yet it is clean and unpolluted by the mire surrounding it. One finds the lotus depicted as the cushion or seat of many meditational deities in Buddhist tantric iconography.

lower existences *ngan-song*, Skt. *durgati* The realms of the animals, anguished spirits, and hells.

Mahākāla *mgon-po nag-po* A wrathful manifestation of *Avalokiteśvara*. See **Avalokiteśvara** and **wrath**.

Mahākāruṇika *thugs-rje chen-po* The thousand-armed form of *Avalo-kiteśvara*. See **Avalokiteśvara**.

major and minor marks *mtshan-dpe*, Skt. *lakṣaṇānuvyañjana* The Buddha-body of Supreme Emanation is characterized by thirty-two major marks and eighty minor marks. These include an array of perfected features of body and speech.

maṇḍala *dkyil-'khor* The Sanskrit word *maṇḍala* conveys a number of meanings—circle, wheel, circumference, totality, assembly, or literary corpus. In the context of our text, this term indicates the central (*dkyil*) and peripheral ('*khor*) meditational deities described in the *tantras*. These deities reside within a celestial palace, which has a perfectly symmetrical design—with four gateways and four main walls composed of five layers of different colors, each of the features corresponding to a particular aspect of the principal deity's (and thereby to the meditator's) pure awareness and purity of perception. The *maṇḍala* thus represents a perfected state of being and perception encompassing all phenomena. The celestial palace itself and the deities within it symbolize the perfected states of the meditator's own awareness, psycho-physical aggregates, elemental properties, sensory and mental processes, etc. These "abodes of the deity" are therefore never perceived as independently existing universes but as manifestations of the pristine cognition of the principal deity being meditated upon.

maṇḍala of offerings *mchod-pa'i maṇḍal* The *maṇḍala* of offerings is a practice in which offerings are visualized and symbolically offered to the spiritual teacher, meditational deity, or Three Precious Jewels.

mantra *sngags* The Sanskrit word *mantra* is an abbreviation of two syllables *mana* and *traya*, respectively meaning "mind" and "protection."

Hence *mantra* literally refers to "protection of the mind." The essential indication here is the protection of the mind from the overwhelming influence of ordinary perceptions and conceptions, which give rise to deluded states of existence, thus inhibiting the full expression of buddha nature. More specifically, *mantra* refers to the pure sound that is the perfected speech of an enlightened being. The aim of the generation-stage practices is the cultivation of the mode of being of the meditational deity, that is to say the transformation of mundane body, speech, and mind into buddha-body, -speech, and -mind. This is supported in ritual practice by the enactment of the hand gestures (*mudrā*), which are the resonance of buddha-body; by *mantra* recitation, which is the resonance of buddha-speech; and by visualization, which is the resonance of buddha-mind.

meditational deity *yi-dam*, Skt. *iṣṭadevatā* Forms or resonances of fully manifest buddhahood whose characteristics are defined or revealed by the specific tantric practices on the basis of which they are visualized. After receiving empowerment and guidance concerning an appropriate meditational deity or *mandala* of deities from an authoritative spiritual teacher, the practitioner of the *tantras* seeks to experientially cultivate union with the qualities of buddha-body, -speech, and -mind through the practice of the generation stage of meditation related to a specific mediational deity or *maṇḍala* of deities. It is essential that the meditational deities should not be perceived as externally existing or independent beings, but rather as a form or resonance of buddha-mind itself.

mental body *yid-lus*, Skt. *manokāya* The noncorporeal body assumed during the intermediate state of rebirth, which is said to have an initial similitude to the physical body of the previous life.

merit *bsod-nams*, Skt. *puṇya* Merit refers to the wholesome tendencies imprinted in the mind as a result of positive and skillful thoughts, words, and actions that ripen in the experience of happiness and well-being.

mind *sems*, Skt. *citta* In Buddhism, mind is defined as a dynamic process, which is simply the awareness of an object or event. Although some Buddhist philosophical schools of thought do identify mind as the essence of being or personal identity, the notion of self or person is not an essential component of the Buddhist concept of mind. In our text an important distinction is made between our ordinary mind (a gross dualizing consciousness) and pure awareness (which is free from the dualistic perceptions of subject and object). See **awareness**, **intrinsic awareness**, and **consciousness**.

Mount Sumeru *ri-rab* Mount Sumeru is the *axis mundi* of Indian cosmology, the center of the world. See **four continents and eight subcontinents**.

natural liberation *rang-grol* In the context of our text, the term *natural liberation* refers to a natural process of recognition of the actual nature of the object, which is free from any form of renunciation or antidote.

natural purity *gnas-su dag-pa/rnam-par dag-pa* In our text, *natural purity* refers to the quiescent, naturally abiding purity of the psycho-physical aggregates, elemental properties, and sensory and mental processes as represented by the peaceful meditational deities.

nirvāṇa *myang-'das* Nirvāṇa (lit. "state beyond sorrow") refers to the permanent cessation of all suffering and the dissonant mental states that cause and perpetuate suffering, along with all misapprehension with regard to the nature of emptiness or actual reality.

nonvirtuous action *mi-dge-ba*, Skt. *akuśala* See **virtuous action**.

obscuration *sgrib-pa*, Skt. *āvaraṇa* There are two main categories of obscurations. First, the obscurations to liberation from the karmically conditioned cycle of existence include not only the conscious states of our deluded mind (such as desire, hatred, jealousy, harmful intent, etc.) but also the psychological tendencies that are imprinted by these states and which serve as seeds for their continuity and recurrence. The second category of obscurations refers to the "propensities for bewildering dualistic appearance," the subtle dispositions and latent tendencies that are deeply ingrained within an individual's psyche and which are the origins of our dualistic perceptions of the phenomenal world and of our own consciousness. A total overcoming of both obscurations marks the attainment of buddhahood.

Oḍḍiyāna *o-rgyan Oḍḍiyāna*, the birthplace of *Padmasambhava*, is the name of an ancient kingdom, probably situated in the remote northwest of the Indian subcontinent, where a large corpus of tantric literature is said to have been propagated in the human world for the first time.

omniscience *thams-cad mkhyen-pa-nyid*, Skt. *sarvajñatā* In a Buddhist context the word is reserved only for the all-knowing pristine cognition of the buddhas. Although the original Sanskrit and Tibetan terms, like their English equivalent, do carry with them the literal connotation of all-knowingness, the principal meaning of the Tibetan word should be understood in terms of a direct and simultaneous perception of the dual aspects of reality, i.e. of the phenomenal aspects (valid only within the relative framework of our ordinary perceptions) and their ultimate nature, emptiness. In other words the term refers primarily to a non-conceptual simultaneous perception of the dual aspects of reality within a single mental act.

Padma family *padma'i rigs*, Skt. *padmakula* One of the five families into which the meditational deities of the Buddha-body of Perfect Resource are subdivided.

past actions *las*, Skt. *karma* The technical term *past actions* refers to the dynamic relationship between actions and their consequences. It includes in its causal aspect both the actual actions (physical, verbal, and mental) and the psychological imprints and tendencies created within the mind by such actions. After the performance of an action a causal chain is maintained within the mental continuum that continues through the present and successive rebirths. Such a karmic potential is activated when it interacts with appropriate circumstances and conditions, thus leading to the fruition of its effects. This dynamic of past actions has two main features: 1) one never experiences the consequences of an action not committed; and 2) the potential of an action once committed is never lost unless obviated by specific remedies. It is also worth bearing in mind that the idea of *karma* in Buddhism cannot be equated with the notion of causality as understood in a strictly deterministic sense.

Peaceful and Wrathful Deities *zhi-khro* This refers to the *maṇḍala* of Peaceful and Wrathful Deities that are expressions of the perfected states of the meditator's own awareness, psycho-physical aggregates, elemental properties, and sensory and mental processes. The Peaceful Deities represent the natural purity of these fundamental components of our being, and the Wrathful Deities represent the transformative aspects of these energies, which bring about the natural transformation of the most enduring and deep-seated expressions of our mundane perceptual states.

perfection stage *rdzogs-rim*, Skt. *sampannakrama* Following the meditative generation of the form of the meditational deity and an approximation of the pristine cognition of the meditational deity during the generation stage, the perfection stage employs techniques for controlling the energy channels, vital energies, and seminal points within the practitioner's transmuted body. The purpose is to make manifest the inner radiance induced by the ever-deepening realization of pristine cognition. The factor that marks the transition from generation stage to perfection stage is the *yogin*'s ability to draw the vital energies into the central channel. See **pristine cognition** and **vital energy**.

pristine cognition *ye-shes*, Skt. *jñāna* The modality of buddha-mind. Although all sentient beings possess the potential for actualizing pristine cognition within their mental continuum, the psychological confusions and deluded tendencies that defile the mind obstruct the natural expression of these inherent potentials, making them appear instead as aspects of mundane consciousness. Buddhist literature mentions five types of pristine cognition that are the quintessential perfected states of our own mental faculties. The pristine cognition of reality's expanse is the natural purity of the aggregate of consciousness, free from delusion; the mirrorlike pristine cognition is the mind to which all the objects of the five senses appear spontaneously, as in a mirror—it is the natural purity of the aggregate of form, free from aversion; the pristine cognition of sameness is the mind that experiences the three different types of feelings (good, bad, and indifferent) as of one taste—it is the natural purity of the aggregate of feeling, free from pride; the pristine cognition of discernment is the mind that accurately identifies names and forms—it is the natural purity of the aggregate of perceptions, free from attachment; and the pristine cognition of accomplishment is the mind that accords with awakened activities and their purposes—it is the natural purity of the aggregate of motivational tendencies, free from envy and self-centered ambition.

pure realm See **buddha field**.

pure realm of the sky-farers *dag-pa'i mkha'-spyod-kyi zhing*, Skt. *khecarīkṣetra* The pure realm or field of the sky-farers represents the level on which the awareness holders are said to abide. See **awareness holder**.

Purification of the Lower Realms *ngan-song sbyong-ba*, Skt. *durgatipariśodhana* This is the *Tantra of the Purification of the Lower*

Realms, which is recited to assist the deceased in avoiding the pitfalls of rebirth as a sentient being trapped in the three lower existences.

Ratna family *rin-chen rigs*, Skt. *ratnakula* One of the five families into which the meditational deities of the Buddha-body of Perfect Resource are subdivided.

realization *rtogs-pa*, Skt. *adhigama* This refers to the spiritual experiences that a practitioner gains through insight into and transformation of the mental continuum while on the path to enlightenment, and to the resultant attainment of liberation or buddhahood.

reality *chos-nyid*, Skt. *dharmatā* In our text the term *reality* refers to the ultimate nature of mind and phenomena.

reality's expanse *chos-dbyings*, Skt. *dharmadhātu* The expanse of actual reality is a synonym for the expanse of emptiness. As such, it indicates both the dimension of the Buddha-body of Reality and the pristine cognition of reality's expanse. See **emptiness**, **Buddha-body of Reality**, and **pristine cognition**.

refuge *skyabs-'gro*, Skt. *śaraṇagamana* This term in Buddhist usage indicates the act of entrusting one's spiritual growth and well-being to the Three Precious Jewels. The Three Precious Jewels are the objects of refuge, and the nature of the refuge sought from each of the three differs. In the Buddha, the fully enlightened teacher, guidance from an enlightened being on a correct path to buddahood is sought; in the sacred teachings, the realizations of the path are sought; and in the monastic community perfect companionship on the path to buddhahood is sought.

Rinpoche *rin-po-che* This term literally means "high in value or esteem," and in ordinary language indicates a precious jewel. By extension, in Tibetan Buddhism, the term has come to refer to an incarnate master who is "high in value" or "most precious." Accordingly, the title *Rinpoche* is widely used by Tibetans to refer to any incarnate spiritual teacher.

Śākyamuni Buddha *śākya thub-pa* Our historical buddha, who is considered to have been the fourth supreme Buddha-body of Emanation to have appeared during this particular aeon. The *Buddha Śākyamuni* is considered by historians to have lived in the sixth century BC and is credited, according to Buddhist tradition, as the progenitor of all the contemporary Buddhist lineages relating to the *sūtras* and certain of those related to the *tantras*, and for the establishment of the early Buddhist monastic community.

seed syllable *yig-'bru*, Skt. *bījākṣara* Generally, this refers to Sanskrit syllables or letters visualized as the quintessential basis from which arise the forms of meditational deities.

selflessness *bdag-med*, Skt. *nairātmya* Selflessness in Buddhist philosophy is understood to imply the lack of inherent existence both in the personality and also in physical and mental phenomena. See **inherent existence**.

sentient being *sems-can/'gro-ba*, Skt. *sattva/gati* In a Buddhist context, the expression *sentient being* has a technical usage that contrasts with the concept of a buddha. The term refers to all beings in cyclic existence and also those who have attained liberation from it but who have not attained fully manifest buddhahood. See **six classes of sentient/living beings**.

six classes of sentient/living beings *'gro-ba rigs-drug*, Skt. *ṣaḍgati* A birth in cyclic existence is characterized as occurring among one or other of the six classes of living beings, depending on the nature and maturity of an individual's past actions. The six classes are: 1) gods, mundane celestial beings whose primary mental state is one of pride or exaltation; 2) antigods, who are predominantly hostile and jealous; 3) human beings, who are influenced by each of the dissonant mental states; 4) animals, who are under the sway of instinct and obfuscation; 5) anguished spirits, who are under the sway of attachment and unsatisfied craving; and 6) the denizens of the hells, who are overwhelmed by hatred, anger, and fear. Since all five dissonant mental states have influence on human beings, it is not inappropriate to look upon all of these conditions also as extrapolations of human psychological states. In our text the primary causes of rebirth in each of these six realms are respectively identified as pride, jealousy, attachment, delusion, miserliness, and hatred.

six dissonant mental states *nyon-mongs drug*, Skt. *satkleśa* In certain instances in our text when the context relates to rebirth among the six classes of beings, this enumeration does not refer to the classical categorization of the six primary dissonant mental states—fundamental ignorance, attachment, aversion, pride, doubt, and dissonant or afflictive views—but to the six poisons that are said to generate rebirth among the six classes of living beings, namely: pride, jealousy, attachment, delusion, miserliness, and hatred.

six intermediate states *bar-do drug* See **intermediate states**.

six realms See **six classes of sentient/living beings**.

six-syllable mantra *yi-ge drug-pa*, Skt. *ṣaḍakṣara* The six-syllable *mantra* (OṂ MAṆI PADME HŪM) is that of *Avalokiteśvara*.

sky-farer *mkha'-spyod-ma*, Skt. *khecarī* See **pure realm of the sky-farers**.

spiritual sibling *mched-grogs/rdo-rje spun-sring* In the context of the *tantras*, six types of spiritual sibling are identified: 1) universal spiritual siblings, i.e. all sentient beings who from beginningless time have been one's parents; 2) spiritual siblings who share the Buddhist teachings; 3) harmonious spiritual siblings who are similar in view and conduct; 4) dear spiritual siblings who share the same spiritual teacher; 5) close spiritual siblings who receive teachings together; and 6) intimate spiritual siblings who receive empowerments together.

spiritual teacher *bla-ma*, Skt. *guru* The original Sanskrit word *guru* literally means "heavy" or "weighty," and by extension "a venerable teacher." The Tibetan equivalent *bla-ma* (pronounced *lama*) means "unsurpassed" or "supreme," indicating that the *guru* is unsurpassed in terms of being the perfect object toward which meritorious activity should be directed. However, it is important to note that specific qualifications are necessary in order to be considered as a spiritual teacher. These qualifications differ according to the level of spiritual practice at which a student adopts a teacher. Ultimately, the *guru* is one's own Buddha nature.

stages of generation and perfection *bskyed-rim*, Skt. *utpattikrama/ rdzogs-rim*, Skt. *sampannakrama* See **generation stage** and **perfection stage**.

stūpa *mchod-rten* A sacred object representative of buddha-mind. *Stūpas* were originally a symbol of the Buddha-body of Reality, constructed in a dome-shape to hold the remains of *Śākyamuni Buddha*. The *stūpas* commonly seen in Tibetan cultural regions are constructed to a specific architectural design, usually in the shape of a dome, raised on a square base of several layers from which rises a multilayered spire. In monasteries and sacred sites, a series of eight *stūpas* is frequently constructed, symbolizing different events in the life of *Śākyamuni Buddha*. Others are extraordinarily large, like those of *Baudhnāth* and *Svayambhū* in Nepal, *Sanchi* in India, and *Borabudor* in Indonesia. The symbolism of the *stūpa* is complex, representing the progression to buddhahood, the five elements, the five pristine cognitions, and so forth. Smaller reliquary *stūpas* are frequently built as a funerary memorial to important spiritual teachers, often enshrining their sacred ashes or embalmed remains.

substantialist views *mtshan-'dzin*, Skt. *lakṣaṇagrahana* The mistaken apprehension that the form, color, and other characteristics assumed by any particular entity have inherent existence. See **inherent existence**.

subtle body *phra-ba'i lus*, Skt. *sūkṣmakāya* In contrast to our gross physical body (composed of flesh, bones, and blood), the subtle body comprises a network of subtle energy channels, vital energies, and seminal points of energy. This form arises as a natural expression of the interaction of the subtle mind and the subtle vital energies on which it depends. See the introductory commentary by HH the Dalai Lama. The most advanced level of subtle body, known in the *tantras* as the pure illusory body, is experienced only when an indivisible unity of buddha-body, -speech, and -mind has been actualized at the conclusion of the generation and perfection stages of meditation. A similitude of such a subtle body can be experienced during the practice of dream yoga, when the level of consciousness is relatively subtle and deep due to the temporary cessation of active sensory processes. The mental body experienced during the intermediate state of rebirth is also a form of subtle body. See also **vital energy**.

suffering *sdug-bsngal*, Skt. *duḥkhatā* In a Buddhist context, the term *suffering* is used in a broad sense and includes not only physical sensations but also mental experiences, that is to say all the essentially unsatisfactory experiences of life in cyclic existence. The various forms of suffering can be categorized into three groups: 1) the suffering of suffering; 2) the suffering of change; and 3) the suffering of pervasive conditioning. The first category refers to all our physical sensations and mental experiences that are self-evident to us as suffering and toward which we have spontaneous feelings of aversion. The second category includes all our experiences that are normally recognized as pleasant and desirable, but which are nonetheless suffering in that persistent indulgence in these always results in the changed attitude of dissatisfaction and boredom. It is only through reflection that the unsatisfactory nature of such experiences can be realized. The third category refers to a basic level of suffering that underlies the round of birth, sickness, old age, and death, and is called the suffering of pervasive conditioning. This suffering serves as the cause of our experiences of the two other classes of suffering. It is called pervasive because it extends to all forms of life in cyclic existence, irrespective of whether or not life-forms are endowed with bodily existence.

sūtra *mdo* The original discourses that *Śākyamuni Buddha* taught publicly to his disciples as a fully ordained monk, consequent to his attainment of buddhahood. The scriptural transmissions of the sacred teachings of Buddhism comprise the canonical *sūtras* and *tantras*, as well as their commentarial literature.

tantra *rgyud* The Sanskrit word *tantra* and its Tibetan equivalent *rgyud* literally mean a "continuum" or "unbroken stream" flowing from the seed of Buddha nature to enlightenment. *Tantra* also refers to the literature or *tantra* texts that expound the meditative practices of the various classes of *tantra*. Because *tantra* includes sophisticated techniques that, unlike the *sūtra* path, enable dissonant mental states (such as desire/attachment and hatred/aversion) to be transmuted, without renunciation or rejection, into states of realization, it is possible for the practitioner to cultivate an uninterrupted continuum between their ordinary initial mind, the advanced mind on the path, and the resultant fully enlightened mind of a Buddha. The successive classes of *tantra* represent stages of ever-decreasing emphasis on external ritual and ever-increasing subtlety of internal meditation, together with an ever-increasing subtlety of the dissonant mental states (attachment in particular), which can be transformed into a blissful experience conjoined with the realization of the actual nature of reality. It is said that, on the basis of the fulfillment of the generation and perfection stages of the *tantras*, fully manifest buddhahood can be attained in a single lifetime.

Those Gone to Bliss *bde-bar gshegs-pa*, Skt. *sugata* An epithet of the buddhas.

three buddha-bodies *sku-gsum*, Skt. *trikāya* See **buddha-body**.

three lower existences *ngan-song gsum*, Skt. *tridurgati* See **lower existences**.

Three Precious Jewels *dkon-mchog gsum*, Skt. *triratna* The Three Precious Jewels comprise the Buddha, the sacred teachings, and the monastic community of monks and nuns. Together these are regarded as the perfect objects in which refuge can be sought from the unsatisfactory nature of life in cyclic existence in general, and particularly from the potential suffering of unfavorable future existences. They are called precious jewels because, like the wish-fulfilling jewels of Indian classical literature, in their metaphorical sense they possess the wish-fulfilling capacity to provide protection from the perils of cyclic existence. See **refuge**.

three times *dus-gsum* The three times are those of past, present, and future.

three world-systems *'jig-rten-gyi khams gsum*, Skt. *tridhātu* According to Buddhism, cyclic existence includes three world-systems, namely: the world-system of desire, the world-system of form, and the world-system of formlessness. Among them, the world-system of desire is a state of existence dominated by sensual experiences, particularly the sensations of suffering and pleasure. It is inhabited by all six classes of sentient beings, including humans and six categories of gods. The world-system of form, in which beings have a comparatively subtle level of consciousness, temporarily devoid of gross sensations of pain and pleasure, is regarded as a state beyond ordinary human existence and inhabited only by gods. Birth in such a realm requires the attainment of one or all of the four meditative concentrations in past lives. Lastly, the world-system of formlessness is regarded as the highest level of rebirth within cyclic existence and a state where an individual's physical faculties exist only as potencies and the individual functions only at the level of consciousness. It is said to be inhabited by those who have mastered the four formless meditative absorptions.

Transcendent Lord *bcom-ldan-'das*, Skt. *bhagavān* According to the Tibetan interpretation, the Sanskrit honorific term *bhagavān*, which has often been translated as "Blessed Lord," indicates a buddha who has: 1) "destroyed" (*bcom*) the four beguiling forces comprising the influence of the psycho-physical aggregates, dissonant mental states, sensual temptations, and mundane death; 2) come to "possess" (*ldan*) the six excellences of lordship, form, glory, fame, pristine cognition, and perseverance; and 3) "transcended" ('*das*) the sufferings of cyclic existence.

transmission *lung*, Skt. *āgama* The Buddhist sacred teachings comprise both experiential realizations and authoritative transmissions. The latter include both the oral teachings and sacred scriptures imparted by the buddhas, as well as the associated commentaries or treatises, which have been transmitted in an uninterrupted lineage or succession from ancient times. In Tibetan Buddhism, it is regarded as essential, if any significant spiritual experience is to be cultivated, that a transmission of both the text and its oral commentary is formally received from an authoritative lineage holder, since a mere theoretical understanding of these topics is not regarded as sufficient.

treasures *gter-ma*, Skt. *nidhi* The Sanskrit *nidhi* (Tib. *gter-ma*), translated in English as "treasure" or "revealed teaching" (*gter-chos*), refers to those sacred Buddhist texts and objects that were concealed in the past in order that they might be protected and revealed in the future for the benefit of posterity.

two extremes *mtha' gnyis*, Skt. *antadvaya* The two extremes of eternalism and nihilism.

universal monarch *khor-lo bsgyur-ba*, Skt. *cakravartin* In the context of Indo-Tibetan Buddhism, the concept of the benign universal monarch or emperor who rules in accordance with the law of the sacred teachings of Buddhism is one that has permeated Buddhist literature since early times. Their appearance in the world is considered a unique and rare event, just as the appearance of a buddha is considered to be unique and rare.

vajra *rdo-rje* In the sense of *rdo-rje pha-lam* (pronounced *dorje phalam*), this term means the diamond, literally "the sovereign among all stones." In Buddhism, however, *rdo-rje* indicates the indestructible reality of buddhahood, which is defined as both imperishable and indivisible. The emblem symbolic of this indestructible reality is also known as *rdo-rje* or *vajra*. This is a scepterlike tantric ritual object usually held in the right palm whenever one is playing a ritual bell. The scepter symbolizes skillful means and the bell discriminative awareness. Simultaneously holding them, one in each palm, represents the perfect union of discriminative awareness and skillful means.

Vajra family *rdo-rje'i rigs,* Skt. *vajrakula* One of the five enlightened families into which the meditational deities of the Buddha-body of Perfect Resource are subdivided.

Vajrapāṇi *phyag-na rdo-rje* The embodiment of the spiritual power and skillful means of all the buddhas as visualized in the form of a meditational deity.

virtuous action *dge-ba*, Skt. *kuśala* Both virtue and its opposite, nonvirtue, are defined in terms of both motivation and the consequences of the action. In order for an action to be defined as either virtuous or nonvirtuous, certain prerequisite features must be present. These are: motivation, the actual execution of the act, and the conclusion. For example, an act is nonvirtuous if it is: 1) motivated by negative intentions;

2) committed by the agent in a sane mind and with full knowledge; and 3) the person derives a sense of satisfaction from having accomplished the act. Such actions can be physical, verbal, or mental. Broadly speaking, nonvirtuous actions are categorized into the following ten types: killing, stealing, and sexual misconduct (which are the three physical actions); lying, divisive speech, harsh speech, and meaningless gossip (which are the four verbal actions); and covetousness, harmful intent, and distorted views (which are the three mental actions). An act is considered virtuous if its doer either passively refrains from the ten recognized types of nonvirtuous action, or actively engages in acts for the sake of others with an altruistic motivation.

vital energy *rlung*, Skt. *vāyu* In the *tantras* and related medical traditions, it is said that there are ten kinds of vital energy or subtle winds that flow through the 72,000 energy channels of the body. These sustain life and include the energies that support various conceptual states within the individual's mind. At the subtlest level, subtle mind and vital energy are thought of as a single entity. The ten kinds of vital energy comprise: five inner vital energies that influence the body's inner motility, and five outer vital energies that have specific effects on the outward motility of the body. The former are the vital energies associated with the five elements (earth, water, fire, wind, space) and their respective colors (yellow, white, red, green, blue). The latter comprise life-breath, muscular movement, digestion, semiotic/vocal movement, and reproduction/waste disposal. The movement of vital energy through the energy channels of the subtle body is refined in the context of the perfection stage of meditation. Ordinarily, in the case of individuals who have not cultivated such practices, both vital energy and subtle mind are diffused via the right and left energy channels and thereby come to permeate the entire network of the body's minor channels. This dissipated vital energy is known as the vital energy of past actions because it is activated by dissonant mental states, and the influence of past actions therefore predominates, obscuring the inner radiance of the subtle mind. However, when the practices of the perfection stage of meditation are applied, the knots that block their combined movement through the energy centers located on the central energy channel are untied and both vital energy and subtle mind enter, abide, and dissolve within the central energy channel of the body; then the nonconceptual inner radiance arises, for which reason it becomes known as the vital energy of pristine cognition. On a physical level, it is important, according to the Tibetan medical tradition, that vital energy remains in balance with bile and phlegm, which are collectively known as the three humors, if sound health is to be maintained.

wind *rlung*, Skt. *vāyu* See **vital energy**.

world-system *'jig-rten-gyi khams*, Skt. *lokadhātu* See **three world-systems**.

wrath *drag-po'i las*, Skt. *maraṇakriyā* The concept of wrath in the context of Buddhist *tantra* should not be understood in terms of even the subtlest egocentric violence or fierceness. Wrath here refers to the natural transformative process of buddha-mind, the aggressive natural transformation of the deep-seated conditioning that underlies mundane deluded consciousness. See also **Peaceful and Wrathful Deities**.

Yama *gshin-rje* See **Yama Dharmarāja**.

Yama Dharmarāja *gshin-rje chos-kyi rgyal-po* The embodiment of the forces of impermanence and the infallible laws of cause and effect. His fierce form is iconographically depicted holding the wheel of life's rebirth processes within his jaws, indicating that the nature of cyclic existence is, in its entirety, bound by impermanence and the laws of cause and effect. In the context of the intermediate state of rebirth he personifies the process of confronting in death the nature of one's past actions during life and, based on the natural laws of cause and effect, he personifies the process of "judgment" that determines the consequential outcome of one's past actions.

yogin *rnal-'byor-pa* According to the Tibetan definition, a *yogin* is defined as "one who seeks to unite with the fundamental nature of reality." In other words, a *yogin* is one who intensively follows the spiritual paths outlined in the generation and perfection stages of meditation.

(For further study and more detailed cross-referencing of Sanskrit and Tibetan terms, please refer to the glossary in our *Tibetan Book of the Dead*, Penguin Classics, 2005.)

Notes

1. In our first complete translation of *The Tibetan Book of the Dead*, Gyurme Dorje has traced the Tibetan literary history of the text and cited sources for further study.
2. See the glossary for a description of the five psycho-physical aggregates and other Buddhist terms used in the commentary. *Ed*.
3. The perspective of *The Tibetan Book of the Dead* is that of Highest Yoga Tantra. *Ed*.
4. Here "substantialist" refers to those who grasp at characteristics, having failed to understand that they lack inherent existence.
5. The so-called "black life channel" is identified with the aorta, in Tibetan medicine, while the "white life channel" is identified with the spinal cord.
6. The inner radiance of the path is that experienced by practitioners and yogins through their spiritual practices prior to death. See glossary under "inner radiance."

7. That is, the central energy channel of the body.

8. Throughout the death process and at each step in the reading of the "Great Liberation by Hearing," the attending lama is expected to enter into those meditative states of awareness that the text describes and which the dying person is encouraged to cultivate. In this way, he or she serves as a support and anchor for the concentration of the dying and the deceased.

9. The two carotid arteries, which induce unconsciousness when pressed, are included among the body's most vulnerable points. Pressure applied at the right moment is said to trap the vital energy and mind together in the central channel, with no possibility of regression or reversal. Correct training in this procedure is of crucial importance, and it is obviously essential that the carotids are not pressed until after the pulse has ceased.

10. The crown fontanelle, at the crown of the head, is regarded as the optimum point of exit for the consciousness of the dying individual.

11. The Tibetan biographical tradition cites many instances of great spiritual masters who at the time of their demise entered into a prolonged experience of this state.

12. The place where the Buddha Śākyamuni is said to have attained buddhahood, below the Bodhi Tree at present-day Bodh Gaya.

Printed in the United States
by Baker & Taylor Publisher Services